~ THE ULTIMATE BOOK OF ~
Christmas Cakes

~THE ULTIMATE BOOK OF ~

Christmas Cakes

~ANNE SMITH~

MEREHURST

I dedicate this book to my husband Clive and my children, Helen and David.
My grateful thanks to Joan Mooney of 'Great Impressions', who so generously gave me the veiners used
throughout the book, and to Jenny and Norma of 'A Piece of Cake' and Pauline Towler of 'Mrs Pickwick'
for their excellent service and support.

First published in 1996 by Merehurst Limited
Ferry House, 51-57 Lacy Road, Putney, London SW15 1PR
Copyright © 1996 Merehurst Limited
ISBN 1 85391 597 1

A catalogue record for this book is available from the British Library.

Edited by Maureen Callis
Designed by Karen Stafford, DQP
Photography by Clive Streeter
Illustrations by Anne Smith
Colour separation by Bright Arts, Hong Kong
Printed in Italy by Olivotto

Acknowledgements

The author would like to thank J.F. Renshaw Limited, Crown Street, Liverpool L8 7RF
for supplying the sugarpaste for this book.
The publishers would like to thank the following suppliers:

Anniversary House
(Cake Decorations) Ltd
Unit 5
Roundways
Elliott Road
Bournemouth BH11 8JJ
Tel: 01202 590222

Cake Art Ltd
Venture Way
Crown Estate
Priorswood
Taunton
Devon TA2 8DE
Tel: 01823 321532

Guy, Paul & Co Ltd
Unit B4
Foundry Way
Little End Road
Eaton Socon
Cambs. PE19 3JH
Tel: 01480 472545

Squires Kitchen
Squires House
3 Waverley Lane
Farnham
Surrey GU9 8BB
Tel: 01252 711749

FOR YOUR INFORMATION

At the front of the book you will find instructions for all the basic icings, pastes and cake preparation.
Cross-references to these are not given in the recipes.
Everything you will need for making and decorating each cake is listed.
A specific equipment list is given for each one, but does not include basic items like rolling pin,
scissors, pencil, ruler, etc., which you would normally have.
Wired flowers must not be inserted directly into the cake – they must be placed in a separate
small cushion of sugarpaste. Gold and silver food colourings are not edible
and therefore need to be removed from the cake before eating.
All cocktail sticks are used as an aid to painting only and *must not* be inserted into cakes.

Contents

INTRODUCTION 6

INTRODUCTION

Christmas is magical time of year and the perfect occasion to make that special cake. This new Christmas cake book will provide ideas and inspiration to cake decorators of all abilities. The wonderful designs range from fun-loving to traditional, and cover all skill levels.

Children will love *Santa's Stocking* bursting with toys, and the *Eskimo Cake* and *Snowman* would be popular for a winter birthday too. *Festive Robins* and *Noel, Noel* are beautiful traditional cakes that will grace any table, while *The Nativity* and *Three Kings* celebrate the religious meaning of Christmas.

All the cakes will be within the scope of those with little or some knowledge and skill in sugarcraft. Some designs, like *A Winter's Scene* sugarpaste collar and *The Nativity*, are for those with more experience. Techniques used include brush embroidery, bas relief, painting and modelling, as well as simple cut-outs, run-outs, frilling and many more.

Beautifully illustrated with stunning photographs, comprehensive step-by-step instructions and photographs, as well as detailed patterns and templates, this book aims to tempt and encourage you to create an edible work of art that truly celebrates the joy of Christmas, and is sure to impress family and friends.

BASIC RECIPES AND TECHNIQUES

Sugarpaste

This paste is used for general purpose decoration throughout this book.

5 tsp gelatine
125ml (4fl oz) liquid glucose
22g (¾oz) glycerine
1kg (2lb) icing (confectioners') sugar, sifted

Sprinkle the gelatine over 4 tablespoons cold water in a small bowl. Leave for 2 to 3 minutes to soften, then stand the bowl over a saucepan of hot water and stir until dissolved and clear. Do not allow the gelatine to boil. Add the glucose and glycerine and stir until melted. Add to the icing sugar and knead to a soft consistency.

Makes 1.25 kg (2½lb)

Modelling paste

This paste is malleable and easily stretched which makes it ideal for bas relief work.

280g (9oz) icing (confectioners') sugar
1 tbsp gum tragacanth
1 tsp liquid glucose
about 315g (10oz) sugarpaste

Sift the icing sugar with the gum tragacanth. Add the glucose and 6 teaspoons cold water and mix well. Knead to form a soft dough, then combine with an equal weight of sugarpaste. If the paste is too dry, knead in a little white vegetable fat (shortening) or egg white. If the paste is sticky, add a little cornflour (cornstarch).

Makes 315 to 345g (10 to 11oz)

Flower paste

There are many variations of the following recipe. This is a reliable one to start with.

440g (14oz) icing (confectioners') sugar
60g (2oz) cornflour (cornstarch)
3 tsp gum tragacanth
2 tsp gelatine
2 tsp liquid glucose
3 tsp white vegetable fat (shortening)
white of 1 egg, string removed

Sift the icing sugar and cornflour into the bowl of a heavy-duty mixer. Sprinkle over the gum tragacanth. Stand the mixer bowl over a large saucepan of boiling water. Cover with a dry cloth and a plate and set aside.

Sprinkle the gelatine over 5 teaspoons cold water in a small bowl. Leave for 2 to 3 minutes to soften.

Half fill a small saucepan with water and heat to just below boiling point. Stand the bowl of sponged gelatine, the liquid glucose in a small container and the beater from the mixer in the water.

Heat gently until the gelatine is clear. Remove the bowl of gelatine from the pan and stir in the glucose and white vegetable fat until the fat has melted.

When the icing sugar feels warm, remove the bowl from the pan of boiling water, dry the bottom and place in the mixer. Remove the beater from the other pan, dry and assemble the mixer. Add the gelatine solution and egg white to the sugar, cover the bowl with a cloth and set the mixer to its slowest speed. Mix until all the ingredients are combined and the paste is a dull beige colour. Increase the speed to maximum and beat for 5 to 10 minutes or until the paste becomes white and stringy. Remove from the bowl and put in a clear polythene bag then in an airtight container.

Refrigerate for at least 24 hours before using

To use the flower paste, cut off a small piece at a time and work with your fingers until it has an elastic consistency. If the paste is dry, add more egg white or white vegetable fat; if the paste is too sticky, add a little more cornflour.

Makes 500g (1lb)

Gelatine paste

1 tbsp gelatine
1 tsp white vegetable fat (shortening)
1 tsp liquid glucose
500g (1lb) icing (confectioners') sugar, sifted

Soak the gelatine in 4 tablespoons cold water as for sugarpaste. Add the white vegetable fat and glucose and stir until melted. Add to the icing sugar and knead together to form a paste, adding a little more water if the paste is too stiff. Pat the surface all over with a little water, then put in a polythene bag and leave in a cool place for 2 hours before using.

Makes 500g (1lb)

To make a plaque simply cut the paste to shape and size with a plaque cutter, or use a scalpel with a template. Decorate as instructed.

NOTE: It is not necessary to refrigerate this paste.

Gum arabic

4 tsp rosewater
1 tsp gelatine crystals

Put the rosewater in a cup standing in a saucepan of hot water. Sprinkle the gelatine into the cup and stir until all the crystals have dissolved; do not allow the mixture to overheat. Strain through a fine sieve lined with muslin, allowing the mixture to drip through gradually. Store in a small glass jar.

NOTE: To make larger quantities, simply increase the quantities in a 4:1 ratio.

Royal icing

1 tbsp albumen powder
500g (1lb) icing (confectioners') sugar, sifted

Add the albumen powder to 5 tablespoons cold water and stir gently; initially the albumen will form lumps but these will disappear. Strain the liquid through a fine strainer into the icing sugar and mix well until the icing forms firm peaks; if using a mixer, this will take about 10 minutes on slow speed. Keep the icing covered with a damp cloth while working to prevent the surface drying out and forming a crust.

Makes 500g (1lb)

NOTE: Any excess icing can be frozen. Re-beat when thawed, until the mixture forms firm peaks again.

Run-out icing

To thin royal icing for run-outs simply add water, or 1 tablespoon albumen powder dissolved in 5 table-spoons water, until it reaches the right consistency: it should find its own level by the count of 10 when a knife is drawn through.

To cover cake with marzipan (almond paste) for royal icing

Unlike a sugarpasted cake, where the top edges and corners are rounded, the edges and sides of a cake to be covered in royal icing need to remain straight and sharp.

Fill any holes or undulations with small pieces of marzipan. Smooth with a knife or smoother so that the surface is level with the cake.

To cover the top of a cake

Roll out the marzipan on a surface dusted with icing (confectioners') sugar. If possible, use marzipan spacers to ensure it is rolled out to an even thickness. Brush the top of the cake with warmed sieved apricot jam (jelly) and place the cake upside down on the marzipan. Cut the marzipan around the cake approximately 2.5cm (1 in) from the edge. As the top of the cake could be slightly convex, there may be a small gap between the cake edge and the surface of the marzipan. Fill this by forcing the excess marzipan flush with the side(s) of the cake using a firm palette knife. Cut away any excess marzipan and smooth the edge with a knife or smoother. When the cake is turned right-way up, the top will be completely flat and the edge sharp. Leave to dry.

To cover the side of a round cake

Measure the circumference and depth of the cake with a piece of string. Cut this measurement from a strip of marzipan. Brush the side of the cake with prepared apricot jam. Roll up the marzipan loosely (like a bandage). Attach the end to the side of the cake and gradually unroll. Cut away any excess and use a smoother to eradicate any fingermarks. Leave to dry.

To cover the sides of a square cake

Measure each side individually and cut the marzipan to size. Brush the sides of the cake with prepared apricot jam and attach the marzipan. Leave to dry.

To coat cake with royal icing

Make the royal icing the day before required as freshly made icing will have too many air bubbles. Usually a cake needs to be iced three or four times to cover well. For the final coat, thin the icing with a little water to ensure a smooth finish.

To ice a round cake

Place the cake on a turntable and apply the icing to the top with a palette knife. Work it from side to side using a paddling movement to eliminate any bubbles. Gradually turn the turntable and work around the top of the cake.

Put the cake on a firm surface at a lower level. Place a straight edge on the furthest point of the cake and pull it across the surface at an angle. If any marks are visible, repeat the process. Clean the cake edge with a sharp kitchen knife using a downwards movement. Leave to dry.

To cover the side, put the cake on a turntable. Apply the icing using the same paddling movement until the entire area has been covered satisfactorily. Place the side scraper on the furthest point of the cake. Rotate the turntable in a continuous movement all the way round, then pull the scraper away. Leave to dry. Clean the top edge of the cake and remove the take-off mark with a sharp knife.

Cover the cake board in the same way.

To ice a square cake

Cover the top as above and leave to dry. Cover two opposite sides and leave to dry. Cover the remaining sides and leave to dry.

To cover cake with marzipan (almond paste) for sugarpasting

Turn the cake upside down so that the base provides a flat top surface. Stick the cake to the board with a little marzipan softened with warm, sieved apricot jam (jelly).

If the edges of the cake do not sit level on the board, make a sausage of marzipan and push into the gaps with a palette knife.

Fill any visible holes and repair any damaged corners with marzipan. Smooth with a palette knife until all the damaged areas are level. Measure the cake with a piece of string: take it up one side, across the top and down the other side. Brush the cake with warm, sieved apricot jam.

Knead the marzipan on a clean, dry work surface until pliable. Dust the surface with icing (confectioners') sugar and roll out the marzipan to the required shape and a little larger than the measured size. Use spacers to keep the thickness of the marzipan uniform.

To cover the cake, lift up the left side of the marzipan and lay it over your right arm. Lift up your arm and drape the marzipan against the side of the cake; the right side of the marzipan should be on the board. Drape over the top of the cake, transfer the marzipan to the left hand and support it while you remove any air bubbles by brushing your right hand across the top of the cake.

Skirt out the corners and, using the flat of your hand, smooth the marzipan to the side(s) of the cake using an upward movement. Use smoothers to eliminate any fingermarks and bumps. Smooth any cracks from the corners and upper edges using the warmth of your hand. Place the flat edge of a cranked palette knife against the cake at the base and cut away the excess marzipan.

To cover cake with sugarpaste

If a cake is to be sugarpasted, it does not have to be covered with marzipan (almond paste) first.

It can be covered with two layers of sugarpaste instead if preferred. The first layer is usually thinner and should be allowed to skin and harden before applying the second layer.

Both layers are applied in the same way.

Knead the sugarpaste and add any colour. Roll out on a surface lightly dusted with icing (confectioners') sugar. Avoid using too much as this will dry the paste and make it crack.

Use spacers to keep the thickness of the paste uniform. Measure the cake and roll out the sugarpaste in the same way as marzipan.

Sterilize the surface of the cake by moistening all over with clear alcohol such as gin, vodka or kirsch. Make sure the entire surface is moist; if there are any dry areas the paste will not stick to the cake and could cause air bubbles.

Lift and drape the paste over the cake using the same technique as for marzipan. Skirt out the corners and smooth out any creases using an upward movement.

Use smoothers to rub over the top and side(s) of the cake and to round the corners.

If any air bubbles have been trapped under the paste, insert a clean needle into the bubble at an angle. Smooth over with your hand to expel the air and rub with a smoother. If the pin hole is still visible, pipe a small dot of royal icing of the same colour into the hole, then wipe away to leave a smooth finish.

Trim away the excess paste with a cranked palette knife. Smooth over the cut area and wipe away any sugar on the board. Leave in a dry place until the sugarpaste has skinned.

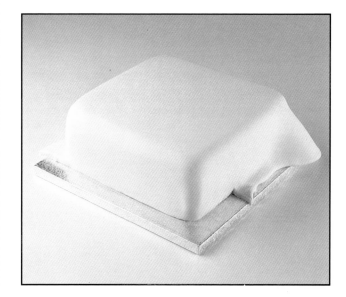

A Child is Born

The dove and figures are all cut-outs. The delicate look is achieved with dusting powders (petal dusts) and a Garrett frill adds the finishing touch.

CAKE AND DECORATIONS
20cm (8 in) round cake
boiled, sieved apricot jam (jelly)
1.25kg (2½lb) marzipan (almond paste)
1.25kg (2½lb) sugarpaste
cornflower blue, lemon, grey, brown and skintone or
    peach dusting powders (petal dusts)
30g (1oz) royal icing
90g (3oz) modelling paste
gum arabic (see page 8)
paprika, melon, tartrazine-free cream, black, brown
    and pink paste colourings
little cornflour (cornstarch)

GARRETT FRILL
30g (1 oz) each flower paste and sugarpaste

EQUIPMENT
28cm (11 in) round cake board
parchment piping bags and No. 1 piping tube (tip)
1m (1yd) pale blue ribbon for base of cake
templates (see below and page 14)
scriber
small ball tool
small scalpel
No. 00 paintbrush
Dresden tool
star cutter
Garrett frill cutter
1m (1yd) gold ribbon for cake board

Enlarge by 125%
on a photocopier

1   Cover the cake with marzipan. Colour the sugarpaste with a little cornflower blue dusting powder until the desired shade is achieved (see Note). Cover the cake and board with the sugarpaste and leave to dry. Attach the cake to the board with a little royal icing. Pipe a snail's trail around the base of the cake with royal icing and the No. 1 tube. Leave to dry, then attach the pale blue ribbon above the piping. Attach the template to the top of the cake and impress the design onto the sugarpaste with the scriber. Keep the template and use as a pattern for the dove, halo and animals.

DOVE

2   WINGS: Roll out the modelling paste very thinly. Cut out the wing. Soften the cut edges with the ball tool, without frilling. Attach to the cake. Mark in the divisions of the feathers with the edge of a sharp knife. Cut the feather shapes with the scalpel. Lift the edges to give a natural effect. Cut out the shape at the top of the wing in slightly thicker paste. Smooth the cut edge with fingers to give a rounded effect. Repeat the process for the second wing and the tail. Thin the inner edge of the shapes so that when the body is attached there will be no visible seam.

3　BODY: Roll out the modelling paste slightly thicker. Using a rolling pin, thin the paste from the upper breast upwards and the area below the feet so that the breast looks more rounded. Smooth the cut edges with fingers and attach to the cake. Indent an eye with the piping tube. Using the Dresden tool, indent two holes in which the feet will be placed. To make the beak, make a tiny elongated cone, indent with the scalpel to separate the upper and lower parts, and attach with gum arabic.

4　FEET: Use a little of the skintone-coloured paste used for the baby (see below). Make a tiny threadlike roll of paste and fold in half, keeping the ends separate. Roll the bottom end to form a Y-shape. Cut to size to fit the bird then roll the cut ends to form claws. Curl and attach to the body. Repeat for the second foot.

5　Colour a small pea-size piece of sugarpaste with lemon dusting powder. Cut out a small star and place above the dove.

BABY

6　Cut out the halo in white modelling paste. Using the ball tool, indent where the baby's head will be placed. Attach to the cake. Colour a small piece of paste flesh-coloured by mixing a little paprika paste colouring with a touch of melon. Make a head with a small currant-size piece of the paste. Indent the eyes with the ball tool, which should push the paste outwards to form a nose. Insert the scriber into the nose to form nostrils. Cut a small line for the mouth. Push up the paste with the Dresden tool to form a lower lip. Pipe on the hair with dark cream royal icing. Attach to the cake with gum arabic.

Actual size

BLANKET

7　Place a piece of tracing paper over the drawing of the blanket. Roll a large grape-size piece of modelling paste into a ball, then flatten slightly in the palms of the hands. Put the paste on the tracing paper and push into place until it resembles the drawing. Using the Dresden tool, thin the bottom edge and mark in the folds. Indent with the ball tool where the animals will be placed. Remove from the tracing paper and attach to the cake with gum arabic.

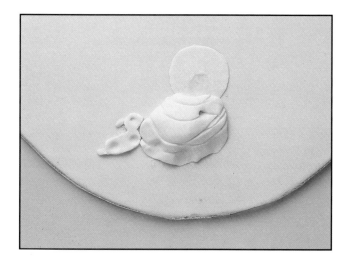

HAY

8　Make small threads around the blanket, using dark cream rolled modelling paste or piped royal icing.

ANIMALS

9　LAMBS: Cut out the main body and rump in white modelling paste, then the ears and legs. Indent an area on the bodies in which to place the back leg, front leg and ears.

CAT AND RABBITS: Cut out the bodies from the neck downwards then the ears and cat's tail in grey and brown modelling paste. Use white paste for the rabbits' tails. Make a small flattened ball for the head and a bigger ball for the rump and attach to the bodies with gum arabic. Indent for the ears and rabbits' tails. Attach to the cake with gum arabic and leave to dry.

TO FINISH

10 To make the mouse, add a little black paste colouring to a small piece of royal icing and pipe an elongated bulb for the body and a small bulb for the head. Pipe an even smaller bulb on the head and pull away to form the ears. Pipe a fine pink line for the tail and feet. Paint on whiskers.

11 Make a light blue by mixing cornflower blue dusting powder and cornflour. Dust the dove's wings and body, between the feathers, under the head, around the feet, etc. Dust the halo lightly. Add cornflour to lemon dusting powder to make a pale yellow and use to dust the area around the crib, halo and star.

12 Add depth to the animals by dusting slightly darker tones around the limbs, under the heads and near the ears. Paint on eyes, noses, etc. Paint eyebrows, lash line and pale pink lips on the baby's face. Dust the cheeks with very light skintone or peach.

13 To make the Garrett frill, knead the flower paste and sugarpaste together well. Cut the frill and attach to the cake with gum arabic. Neaten the finish by piping small dots along the top edge. Dust the bottom edge of the frill with cornflower blue dusting powder mixed with cornflour until the exact shade of the cake has been achieved. Fix the ribbon around the cake board.

NOTE: When colouring sugarpaste, cut through the bulk of the sugarpaste to ensure the colour has been thoroughly mixed. If it hasn't a streaky effect will be seen. However, if you require a marbled look, which can be effective, roll out the paste at this stage.

The Nativity

The stunning effect on this cake is created with a sunken plaque in the centre,
painted and built up with cut-outs, surrounded by a modelled stable 'built' on top of the cake.

CAKE AND DECORATIONS

20cm (8 in) square cake
1kg (2lb) marzipan (almond paste)
boiled, sieved apricot jam (jelly)
1kg (2lb) bought dark blueberry sugarpaste
gelatine paste (see page 8)
blueberry, opaque white, yellow, tangerine, dark brown,
    tartrazine-free cream, black, chestnut, paprika,
    melon and gooseberry green paste colourings
250g (8oz) modelling paste
pale yellow, light and dark brown dusting powders
    (petal dusts)
gum arabic (see page 8)
250g (8oz) white sugarpaste

EQUIPMENT

smoother
absorbent kitchen paper
10cm (4 in) plaque cutter
templates (see pages 18, 19, 88 and 89)
scriber
No. 00 paintbrush
clay gun
scalpel
modelling tool
No. 1 piping tube (tip)
medium round petalled blossom cutter
small piece of foam
28cm (11 in) square cake board
1.5m (1½yd) sandy-brown ribbon for cake board

1   Cut out a 10cm (4in) square section 1.5cm (¾ in) deep from the centre of the cake. Use a sharp kitchen knife and keep the sides and corners of the cavity as straight and sharply angled as possible, as the square will diminish in size and the corners and edges become rounded when covered with marzipan and sugarpaste.

2   Roll out the marzipan and use to cover the cake. Drape it over the cake, make a slit in the centre and gently ease it into the cavity. Use a smoother to ensure all the edges and corners are as flat and sharp as possible. It does not matter if the base is not completely covered as it will be covered with a plaque. Repeat with the blue sugarpaste and leave to dry.

PLAQUE

3   Make a template of the base of the hollow with absorbent kitchen paper so that you can get right into the corners. Using the template and cutter, make a gelatine plaque. Leave to dry.

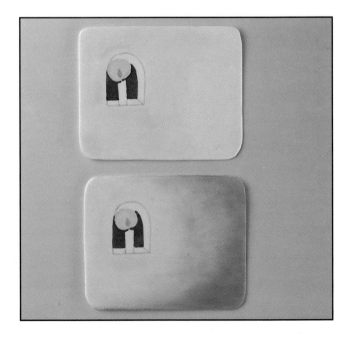

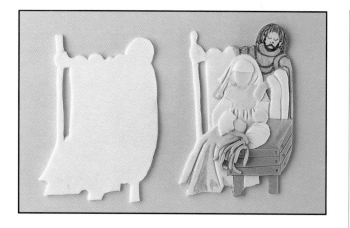

Actual size

4 Using the base plaque template, scribe the window and candle onto the gelatine plaque. Paint the dark blue sky background around the candle, the white candle, the halo of light around the candle and the flame, using paste colourings. Leave to dry. Lightly dust the immediate area around the window a pale yellow, graduating to a lighter brown then a darker brown, until the corners of the room furthest away from the light are quite deep in colour. Apply some sticky 'glue' (see Note page 21) to the base of the hollow and place the finished plaque in position.

STABLE

5 Colour a small grape-size piece of modelling paste a medium brown wood colour. Roll it out quite thinly and cut out the two upright supports. Trim away the excess paste at the base of each support and position on each side of the plaque. Attach with gum arabic.

6 Make a paper template of the floor area of the stable. Colour a small piece of modelling paste a dark straw colour with cream, brown and black paste colourings. Roll it out, position the template and cut out the floor. Attach in position with gum arabic.

7 Colour 60g (2oz) modelling paste as above, but with only the merest touch of black. Push a little of this paste through the clay gun to create the straw.

BORDER DETAIL actual size

Attach at the top and base of the uprights with gum arabic, and to the corners of the plaque if there are any gaps between it and the base of the hollow.

FIGURES

8 Make templates in fine card of Mary and Joseph and the cow. Roll out a large grape-size piece of white modelling paste to 2.5mm (¹/₈ in) thick. Place the template of Mary and Joseph on the paste and cut around it with the scalpel. Smooth all the cut edges and leave to dry. Colour a small piece of the paste chestnut and cut out the cow in the same way. Leave to dry.

9 Using the individual template pieces, build up the figures with cut modelling paste and attach with sticky 'glue', starting with background areas first. Paint the figure of Joseph onto the cut-out, except for the arm that is placed on Mary's shoulder. Cut this out in white paste and attach to the cut-out. Indent the folds in the sleeve with the modelling tool.

10 Cut out Mary's veil in white paste and her dress in blue. Indent the folds in the clothing as above. Attach her upper sleeve and place the lower sleeve (from elbow to wrist) on top of her dress so that it appears to come forward. Colour a small grape-size piece of paste a skintone colour with a little paprika and a slight touch of melon. Cut out Mary's face and hand. Cut a further piece of white paste for the part of the veil that covers her forehead. Attach it to the edges of the face so that it appears to come forward.

11 To make the crib, colour 60g (2oz) paste a light brown wood colour and roll out 2.5mm (¹/₈ in) thick. Gradually roll out the paste for the side of the crib so that it is as thin as the paste used for Joseph's sleeve. Cut out the side and attach to the cut-out. Indent the line of the wood with the back of a knife and indent the nail heads with the icing tube. Roll a small skintone ball of

paste for the baby's head and flatten between the fingers. Position in the crib. Push some of the straw coloured paste through the clay gun and attach it to the front and sides of the crib.

12 To make the baby's body, form a small ball in white paste. Roll with the fingers into a short sausage shape that is thicker at one end, gradually becoming smaller and more tapered at the neck edge. Indent the folds with the base of the icing tube. Put in the crib.

13 Paint in the details of the faces, fingers, etc. and emphasise the folds in the clothing with paste colourings and/or dusting powders. Complete the cow and fencing using the same technique.

14 Cut out a brick shape 5mm (¹/₄ in) thick and place in the corner of the plaque under the window. Attach with sticky 'glue'. Place the cow cut-out on top of the brick so that it is completely hidden and attach with sticky 'glue'. Place a larger and thicker brick in a more central position and attach Mary, Joseph and the crib.

ROOF

15 Colour 60g (2oz) paste a chestnut/brick colour. Make the template in fine card. Roll out the paste as thinly as possible and cut around the template with the scalpel. Smooth the cut edges with fingers and leave to dry. Mark the bricks with the paintbrush and paint the wooden beams showing through the hole a darker brown. Paint in the wooden beams on the underside of the cut-out. Make short thin strokes in varying directions between the beams, for the straw.

16 Make some straw with the clay gun. Separate the layers while attached to the nozzle of the gun, so that the pieces are not quite as chunky. Attach to the bottom edge of the roof, then gradually work upwards, following the curved outline.

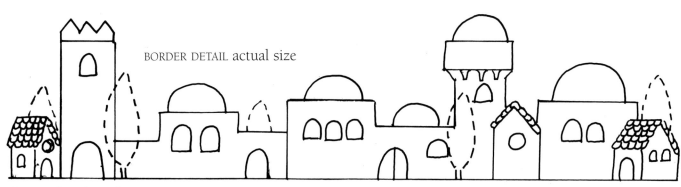

BORDER DETAIL actual size

Cut out dotted area for trees

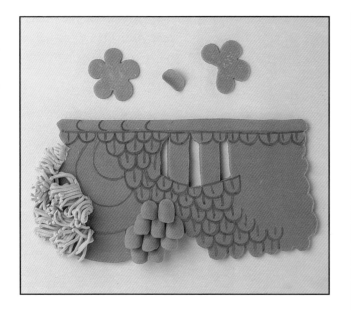

FENCE

18 Make two side fences and uprights in the same coloured paste used for the crib. Indent the line of the wood as step 11 and make indents for the nail heads with the icing tube. Leave to dry thoroughly as these will need to support the weight of the roof.

TO ASSEMBLE

19 Apply sticky 'glue' to one edge of the fence and place this edge on the cake. Cut out two single strips of fencing and place either side of the fence to add extra support. Leave until completely dry and very firm. Make some more 'glue' and apply to the upper edge of the fence. Place the upright supports on this edge, support with foam and leave to dry. Make straw as before and arrange around the figures inside the stable, over the floor and at the base of the supports.

17 To make the bricks, roll out the same coloured paste fairly thinly. Cut out the blossom shape, then use the scalpel to cut out one of the petals. Flatten the cut edge between the fingers to soften, then curve the end of the petal over the paintbrush or modelling tool. Attach to the bottom edge of the roof. Keep adding tiles in this way, gradually working across and upwards.

20 To attach the roof, which is quite heavy, will need extra support. Cut a strip of paste 11cm (4½ in) long, 2.5mm (⅛ in) thick, and 5mm (¼ in) wide. Attach it to the cake with gum arabic where the back edge of the roof is to be placed. Cut two triangular supports, the same thickness, and attach to either side of the strip

with gum arabic. Apply some 'glue' to each triangular support. Attach straw to the top of each upright. Make some straw-coloured 'glue' and place on top of the straw. Attach the roof to all these sticky edges and leave until completely dry and very firm. Make some straw and attach to each triangular support and along the inside roof edge where it is attached to the thick strip.

NOTE: To make sticky 'glue', mix gum arabic with a little of the same coloured modelling paste. Blend together with a palette knife until the paste is very soft and sticky.

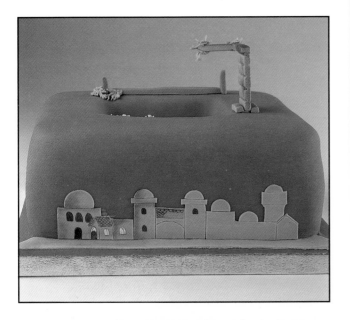

TO FINISH

21 Colour the white sugarpaste dark straw/sand as before and use to cover the cake board. Colour 60g (2oz) modelling paste the same colour and roll out thinly. Cut out the border outlines. Trace the border detail and use as a pattern to indent the lines between the houses and towers with the back of a knife. Use the base of the piping tube to cut out a circular shape, cut in half and attach to the houses with 'glue' for domes. Leave to dry. Paint on the windows, doors, roofs, etc. with paste colourings. Carefully dust shadows onto the houses with dark brown dusting powder to create depth. For the lighted windows, paint with opaque white, leave to dry, then paint with pale yellow.

22 Colour a large grape-size piece of modelling paste with gooseberry green paste colouring and cut out the trees using the dotted shape on the border detail as a pattern. Attach between the houses and paint on the trunks with dark brown paste colouring. Attach the border to the cake.

23 Paint small stars on the sky area using opaque white and pale yellow as above. Cut out a larger star in yellow modelling paste and attach above the crib. Form some tiny balls of different coloured pastes and flatten on a board until really thin. Attach to the cake in front of the stable to represent pebbles. Leave to dry. Attach the cake very carefully to the board with marzipan mixed with apricot jam. Fix the ribbon around the board.

Christmas Garland

This winter's scene is painted directly onto the sugarpaste and enhanced by cut-out flowers.

CAKE AND DECORATIONS
20cm (8 in) round cake
boiled, sieved apricot jam (jelly)
1.25kg (2¹/₂lb) marzipan (almond paste)
1.25kg (2¹/₂lb) white sugarpaste
90g (3oz) royal icing
chestnut, tartrazine-free cream, dark brown, Christmas,
    gooseberry and moss green, black, yellow and melon
    paste colourings
light brown, forest and light green, black, red, pink and
    burgundy dusting powders (petal dusts)
125g (4oz) flower paste
gum arabic (see page 8)
strong red powder colour

EQUIPMENT
28cm (11 in) round cake board
parchment piping bags and No. 1 piping tube (tip)
template (see page 89)
scriber
No. 00 paintbrush
small leaf cutter
Dresden tool
small and very small ball tools
Christmas rose cutter
rose petal veiner
yellow stamens
tweezers
cocktail sticks (toothpicks)
1m (1yd) each thin green and red ribbon for cake base
1m (1yd) green ribbon for cake board

1   Marzipan the cake, then cover the cake and board with sugarpaste; leave to dry. Attach the cake to the board with a little royal icing. Pipe a fine snail's trail around the base of the cake with firm peak royal icing and the No. 1 piping tube.

2   Position the template on the top of the cake and impress the design onto the sugarpaste with the scriber. Carefully paint on the house and trees, etc., taking care to keep the brush as dry as possible. Keep the colours fairly muted in order to keep the scene in the background – if they are too strong, the scene will appear to be on the same level as the flowers. Leave to dry.

3   Dust the area around the house with light brown; this will highlight the snow on the roof and help to lead the scene into the top edges of the spray, thus forming a circle.

SPRAY

4   Start on the flowers and leaves furthest away and gradually work forward.
MAIN STEMS: Colour a small, grape-size piece of flower paste chestnut and roll into a long strand. Cut in half with a sharp knife and fix in place with gum arabic. Colour some royal icing the same colour and pipe on the finer strands and ferns.

5   LEAVES: Colour a grape-size piece of flower paste with tartrazine-free cream paste colouring. Roll out thinly and cut out small leaves. Indent the central vein with the Dresden tool, soften the edges with the small ball tool, then twist to create a natural effect. Fix in place with gum arabic.

6   HOLLY LEAVES: Colour a walnut-size piece of flower paste dark green with Christmas green and a little black paste colourings. Using the tracing as a template, cut out the holly shapes. Indent the veins and ball the edges as above. Leave to dry. Dust the edges with forest green and black dusting powders.

Flash the leaves over a steaming kettle to glaze. Fix in place with a little royal icing.

7   POINSETTIA LEAVES: Colour a large grape-size piece of flower paste light green with gooseberry green and a little black paste colourings. Using the tracing as a template, cut out the leaves. Dust the edges with forest green and black, then with red mixed with a little forest green to form a dirty red. Steam lightly as above and fix in place with a little royal icing.

8   CHRISTMAS ROSE: Roll out a small grape-size piece of white flower paste thinly and cut out five petals with the rose cutter, then vein to give the desired effect. Leave to dry. Dust the edges pink and the base with light green, working from the base of the petal upwards and outwards. Attach the petals to the cake with a little royal icing. Colour a little royal icing the same colour as the stamens and pipe a small bulb in the centre of the flower. Cut a bunch of stamens to length, hold together firmly and insert as a complete unit into the bulb of icing. Use tweezers to arrange the stamens so that they radiate outwards and create a natural effect.

9   POINSETTIA: Colour a large walnut-size piece of paste with strong red powder colour. Roll out thinly and cut out each petal, using the tracing as a template. Indent the veins and ball the edges (see step 5). Place the petals on the cake and twist into shape, arranging them between the leaves and over the Christmas rose so that the flower appears to come forward. Leave to dry. Dust one edge with burgundy dusting powder. Position, then fix in place with royal icing. Dust the centre of the flower with red and

burgundy mixed. Make tiny balls of gooseberry green flower paste, hollow out the centre with the cocktail stick and insert a ball of red paste. Fix in the centre of the flower with royal icing.

10   BERRIES: Colour small amounts of flower paste dark red, mid red, light red and red/green. Form a small oval ball, then insert a cocktail stick into the top of the berry. Leave to dry. Insert a tiny piece of black flower paste into the formed hole and nip the end with tweezers to give a rough effect. Attach to the piped stems with royal icing.

TO COMPLETE

11   Attach thin red and green ribbons to the base of the cake. Fix a green ribbon around the cake board. If wished, attach a small spray of leaves and berries (made as above) to the board.

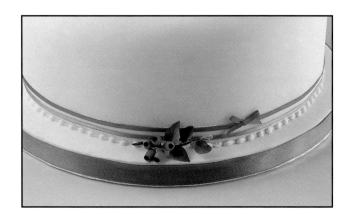

Three Kings

Run-out kings and collars make a beautifully simple royal-iced cake.

CAKE AND DECORATIONS
20 x 15cm (8 x 6 in) oval cake
boiled, sieved apricot jam (jelly)
1.25kg (2¹/₂lb) marzipan (almond paste)
1.5kg (3lb) royal icing
extra albumen powder (optional)
iced mint green and blueberry food colourings
gold food colouring

EQUIPMENT
25 x 20cm (10 x 8 in) oval cake board
straight edge and side scraper
templates (see below and page 87)
glass or perspex
double-sided tape
waxed paper or run-out film
parchment piping bags and No. 1 piping tube (tip)
anglepoise lamp
No. 00 paintbrush
cranked palette knife
1m (1yd) pale blue ribbon for cake board

Enlarge by
143% on a
photocopier

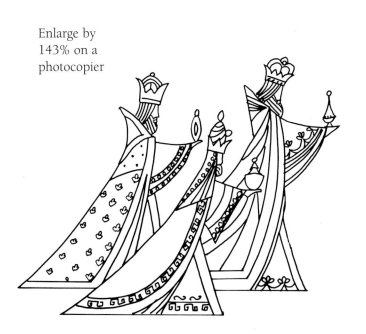

1   Marzipan the cake, then cover the cake and board with royal icing; leave to dry. Attach the cake to the board with a little royal icing.

KINGS
2   Attach the template to the glass or perspex with double-sided tape. Cover with waxed paper or run-out film, ensuring that there are no creases, and secure with double-sided tape or spray glue.

3   Outline the figures with the No. 1 tube and royal icing. Set aside a little icing for piping the collars (see step 4), then thin the remainder with water or dissolved albumen (see page 8). Colour a little of the icing with *a touch* of mint green food colouring and a little with *a touch* of blueberry. Leave the rest white. Flood the figures, working from the back forwards. Dry each area under the lamp to ensure it dries with a slight sheen. Leave to dry completely, then paint the patterns on the clothing with a fine, fairly dry brush. Paint in the gold areas. Leave to dry.

COLLARS

4   Prepare the two collar templates as before. Outline each section with the reserved stiff peak white royal icing and pipe the straight lines on the open sections. Flood each section with thinned white royal icing and dry under the lamp. Pipe dots between the straight lines as shown. Leave to dry, then paint the tips gold. Pipe dots around each section. Leave to dry completely.

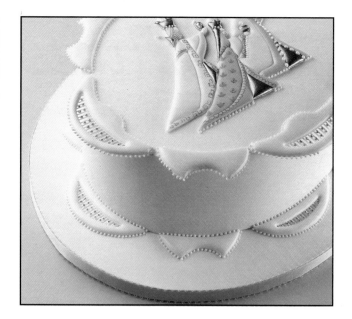

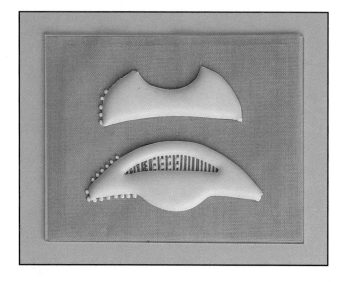

TO FINISH

5   Remove the base collar sections from the waxed paper with the cranked palette knife and attach to the board with dots of royal icing. Remove the kings from the waxed paper, position on top of the cake and fix with royal icing. Finally, carefully remove and attach the upper collar sections to the edge of the cake, using a little more royal icing for support. Fix the ribbon around the cake board.

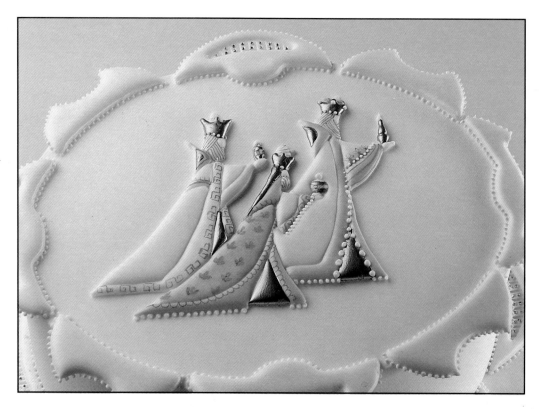

Eskimo Cake

*Fun for a children's Christmas party or the young at heart and quite straightforward to make.
The figures are moulded from modelling paste and are within the scope of
less experienced cake decorators.*

CAKE AND DECORATIONS
*1kg (2lb) white sugarpaste
20cm (8 in) round cake
boiled, sieved apricot jam (jelly)
1.25kg (2½lb) marzipan (almond paste)
1.25kg (2½lb) bought red sugarpaste
125g (4oz) royal icing
blueberry, paprika, melon, black, light and dark
    brown and paprika paste colourings
90g (3oz) modelling paste or Fimo
cornflour (cornstarch) for dusting
pillar box red and black strong powder colours
gum arabic (see page 8)*

EQUIPMENT
*28cm (11 in) round cake board
parchment piping bag and No. 1 piping tube (tip)
18cm (7 in) and 2.5cm (1 in) round biscuit (cookie)
    cutters
smoother
template (see page 92)
scalpel
No. 00 paintbrush
doll's head or face mould
Dresden tool
scriber
small ball tool
piece of dowel
small pieces of foam
palette knife
cocktail stick (toothpick)
tea-strainer
1m (1yd) picot-edged red ribbon for cake board*

1   Cover the cake board with white sugarpaste; leave to dry. Marzipan the cake, then cover with red sugarpaste; leave to dry. Attach the cake to the board with a little royal icing and pipe a snail's trail around the base.

2   Roll out 90g (3 oz) white sugarpaste thinly and cut out an 18cm (7 in) circle with the biscuit cutter, or use the solid line on the template as a pattern. Place on top of the cake and smooth the cut edge with the smoother so that it won't be noticeable when covered with the next layer of paste.

3   Roll out the remaining white sugarpaste and cut carefully round the outer shaped edge of the template. Smooth the shape to make a rounded edge, then place over the cake. Remove the inner circle with the biscuit cutter, then make a sharp jagged edge with a knife.

4   Paint the area beside the inner cut edge, 2.5cm (1 in) in all round, with blueberry paste colouring. Paint in little waves with different tones of blue to give depth. Make small white waves by removing the blue with a slightly wet brush – not too wet or it will melt the sugar.

5 Cut out the central iceberg from the remaining piece of sugarpaste, leaving the cut edges sharp. Place in position in the centre of the cake. Cut out a hole with the small biscuit cutter. Leave to dry, then carefully paint the base of the hole black.

ESKIMO

6 HEAD: To make the mould, press the face of the doll or face mould into a large grape-size piece of modelling paste or Fimo, making sure there are no creases as this will mar the face when the mould is dry. Leave to dry then remove from mould or, if using Fimo, harden in the oven as directed. To make the head, colour a large grape-size piece of modelling paste flesh-coloured with a little paprika and a slight touch of melon paste colourings. Roll between the palms of the hands until no creases are visible. Dust the mould and the paste with cornflour so that the paste can be easily removed when shaped. Push the paste into the mould, pressing it into the features. Remove from the mould and emphasise the features. Slant the eyes slightly upwards with the Dresden tool and create two nostrils with the point of the scriber. Emphasise the eyes by indenting the area above with the small ball tool, creating a brow line. Open the mouth by cutting across the lips with the scalpel and inserting the flattened end of the Dresden tool. Curl up the edges of the mouth to create a smile, by indenting with the Dresden tool.

7 CLOTHES: Colour 60g (2oz) modelling paste strong red with pillar box red powder colour.

Trousers: Roll a walnut-size piece of paste into a flat sausage. Cut into the lower half of the sausage to create two legs. Smooth the cut edges and round the bottom of the cuts at the ankles. Sharpen the dowel to a point and insert into the ankles to create an opening in which to place the feet. Bend the knees. Prop up the shape on a piece of foam so that it leans forward and leave to dry.

Jacket: Take another small walnut-size piece of paste and shape into a cone. Open up the cone with the dowel until the jacket is the correct size and shape. Keep placing over the trousers until the correct size is achieved.

Sleeves: Take two small grape-size pieces of paste, roll each into a sausage and open up the cuffs as for the trousers. Bend the sleeve and cut away the inner part at the shoulder so that it will sit neatly on the jacket and not stand away from the body in an unnatural manner.

Hat: Make a small flattish cone. Using the fingers, keep pinching and opening up the cone so that it becomes bigger. Keep placing the cone on the eskimo's head until it is the right size. Pinch in the excess paste at the back of the hat and trim away. Glue in place.

8 TO ASSEMBLE: Make some strong sticky 'glue' by mixing gum arabic with a little red modelling paste. Using the palette knife, glue the jacket to the trousers, the head to the jacket and the arms to the shoulders.

Mitts: Roll a pea-size piece of light brown paste into a ball, then shape into a cone. Flatten and cut out a V-section from the side of the mitt for the thumb. Touch the point of the thumb to round off and bend the hand. Insert the pointed end into the sleeve and attach with 'glue'. Make three tiny holly leaves and berries and attach to one mitt.

Shoes: Take a grape-size piece of black paste (see step 10), roll into a sausage shape, flatten one end and shape to make one left foot and one right. Bend the shoes in half. To form the heel, place the cocktail stick across the bottom of the sole and indent a line. Round off the heel at the back of the shoe. Attach to the end of the trouser leg with 'glue'.

9 Outline the eyes and paint on eyebrows with light brown paste colouring. Colour the lips with paprika. Paint in the hair using dark brown paste colouring. Push some white modelling paste through the tea-strainer to form the fur on the clothes. Glue in place.

PENGUIN

10 BODY: Set aside a small grape-size piece of modelling paste. Colour the rest black with strong powder colour. Take a walnut-size piece of paste and form a large rounded sausage. Make an impression with the little fingers to create a division between the head and the body. Make a cut for the tail, pinch between thumb and fore-finger and lift upwards. Flatten the base of the body.

BIB: Roll a large pea-size piece of white modelling paste into a fat sausage, then flatten with fingers until an oval shape is formed. Thin around the edge as much as possible. Glue in place under the neck and tuck under the body.

FLIPPERS: Roll two small pea-size pieces of black paste into cones, flatten and shape into flippers, upturning the end. Attach to the body with black sticky 'glue'.

FEET: Colour most of the reserved modelling paste pale melon. Roll all but a pea-size piece into a small sausage, then flatten. Make a cut at each end and round off each section. Make two further cuts to form three toes at the front of each section. Round off the cut points as before. Glue in place underneath the body.

EYES: Make two tiny balls in white paste, flatten and glue to the face to form eyes. Paint in dark brown circles.

BEAK: Make a small cone with the reserved melon paste. Flatten slightly, then cut a line around the cone with the scalpel to form upper and lower beaks. Glue in place.

TO FINISH

11 When dry, attach the figures to the top of the cake with a little royal icing. Make two tiny fish with modelling paste, paint on some scales and attach with royal icing. Roll some brown modelling paste very thinly to form a fishing rod and glue in place on the cake. Fix the ribbon around the cake board.

Snowman

Another cake the children will love.
Replace 'Noel' with the child's name and it would make a good cake
for a winter birthday, too. The technique used is bas relief.

CAKE AND DECORATIONS

20cm (8 in) round cake
boiled, sieved apricot jam (jelly)
1.25kg (2¹/₂lb) marzipan (almond paste)
1.5kg (3lb) sugarpaste
60g (2oz) royal icing
Christmas and spruce green, black, tangerine, dark
    brown, cream, yellow, paprika and red paste
    colourings
90g (3oz) modelling paste
gum arabic (see page 8)
nutkin, ice blue and cornflower blue dusting powders
    (petal dusts)

GARRETT FRILL

30g (1oz) each flower paste and sugarpaste

EQUIPMENT

28cm (11 in) round cake board
template (see right)
scriber
No. 1 paintbrush
small ball tools
Dresden tool
cocktail stick (toothpick)
scalpel
new dishcloth
flexi mat
parchment piping bags and No. 1 piping tube (tip)
Garrett frill cutter
tiny holly cutter
alphabet cutters for NOEL
1m (1yd) dark green ribbon for cake board

1   Marzipan the cake then cover the cake and board with sugarpaste; leave to dry. Attach the cake to the board with a little royal icing. Position the template on the cake and scribe the design onto the sugarpaste.

2   Paint the fir trees with Christmas green paste colouring, leave to dry then paint on darker green shadows to create the foliage. Paint the other trees with spruce green, leave to dry, then paint on the branches in a darker tone.

3   Cover the design with tracing paper and use as a guide when making the head, body, etc., to help form the correct shape.

Actual size

SNOWMAN

4 HEAD: Roll a grape-size piece of modelling paste between the palms of the hands and flatten. Place on the tracing paper and pinch and push into shape. Attach to the cake with gum arabic.

5 BODY: Roll a piece of modelling paste, roughly the size of a small plum, into a ball, then form a cone and flatten. Shape and position below the head as above. Indent with the ball tool where the arms, rabbit, racoon and snowballs are to be placed. Indent the eyes, nose and buttonholes with the end of the paintbrush. Mark the creases around the eyes and cheeks with the Dresden tool. Create holes in which to place the teeth with the cocktail stick. Colour a grape-size piece of paste black. Roll small balls of paste and insert into the eye sockets and buttonholes. Make tiny balls of black paste and insert into the holes made for the teeth. Colour a small piece of paste tangerine, roll into a ball, then into an elongated cone. Mark three or four grooves with the scalpel, upturn the tip and place in the nose socket.

6 SCARF: Roll out a small piece of white modelling paste and cut out the scarf shapes (A, B and C). Emboss by texturing with the dishcloth (see Santa's Stocking, page 65). Shape and position (A) as before.

7 ARMS: Roll a grape-size piece of modelling paste into a smooth sausage shape. Bend, mark the creases for the wrist and bend in the arm and pinch the elbow. For the small arm, form an elongated cone. Attach the scarf (B) around the neck and finally section (C).

8 HAT: Colour a large grape-size piece of modelling paste black. Roll out a little, not too thin, and cut out the back hat brim. Attach to the cake with gum arabic. Cut out the remaining hat brim shapes and cover with flexi mat so that the paste does not dry out. Roll the remaining paste into a fat sausage, flatten and place on the traced design. Cut to shape. Smooth and round any cut edges with fingers. Place against the top of the head. Roll out a small piece of white paste and, using the template, cut out the hat band and attach with gum arabic. Place the remaining hat brim shapes in position to form one continuous shape. Pipe run-out icing (see page 8) onto the top of the hat as shown.

RABBIT

9 Colour a large grape-size piece of modelling paste with a little dark brown paste colouring. Roll two-thirds into a ball for the main body, then form a cone. Indent the line for the hip and a channel where the arm will be placed with the Dresden tool. Roll out a tiny piece of the paste and cut out a triangular shape for the back ear. Fix in place with gum arabic.

10 Roll a grape-size piece of the paste into a ball for the head, then form a cone. Indent an eye with the cocktail stick or tiny ball tool. Make a small hole in which to place the other ear.

11 To make the ear, make a tiny cone with the dark brown paste. Add a little cream colouring to a pea-size piece of brown paste and make a smaller cone. Flatten both cones and place one on top of the other. Flatten again. Pinch the pastes at the base of the ear together and trim away the excess at the back. Fix in position on the head with gum arabic.

12 Make a small ball of black paste and insert into the eye socket. Roll a grape-size piece of dark brown paste into a long thin sausage for the arm and bend to form a gentle curve.

RACOON & MOUSE

13 Repeat steps 9, 10, 11 and 12. Use mixed cream and brown paste colourings for the racoon and grey for the mouse. Make the racoon's tail the same way as his arms.

BIRDS

14 Colour a pea-size piece of paste brown using nutkin dusting powder and a similar size piece of paste pale blue using ice blue dusting powder. Roll out thinly. Cut out the back wing and attach to the cake, then cut out the head, body and tail as one shape and attach. Cut out the upper wing. Attach to the bird by the inner edge only so that the feathers can be lifted up slightly to give movement. Roll a tiny ball, flatten and place on the head to give a 3D effect. Indent an eye using the No. 1 piping tube. Repeat for the second bird.

TO FINISH

15 Place paste snowballs at the base of the snowman and for the rabbit's tail. Paint stripes on the scarf and details on the animals as shown. Dust shadows on the animals. Dust the sky a pale blue. Paint some fine brown lines on the foreground and, when dry, dust blue to create depth. Pipe tiny beaks on the birds with a little yellow royal icing and a tail and feet on the mouse with pale paprika. Pipe noses on the animals with black royal icing. Pipe snow on the fir trees.

16 Pipe a snail's trail around the base of the cake with white royal icing. To make the Garrett frill, knead the two pastes together well. Cut the frill and attach to the cake. Pipe tiny dots of icing on the top edge to neaten.

17 Colour a grape-size piece of modelling paste with Christmas green. Roll out thinly and cut out tiny holly shapes with the cutter. Place at the top of each frill, as shown, and pipe some red berries between the leaves. Place a holly leaf in the mouth of the bluebird.

18 Colour a little modelling paste with Christmas green paste colouring. Roll out and stamp out Noel with alphabet cutters. Attach to the cake with gum arabic. Fix the ribbon around the cake board.

Christmas Manger

Cut-work has been used to decorate this cake.
It is a very simple technique and within the scope of any beginner.

CAKE AND DECORATIONS

20 x 15cm (8 x 6 in) oval cake
boiled, sieved apricot jam (jelly)
1kg (2lb) marzipan (almond paste)
1kg (2lb) bought marine blue sugarpaste
blueberry, chestnut, dark brown, mint and spruce
　　green, black and cream paste colourings
125g (4oz) royal icing
60g (2oz) flower paste
gum arabic (see page 8)
lemon, dark warm brown, navy, emerald green and
　　cornflower blue dusting powders (petal dusts)
strong red powder colour

GARRETT FRILL

45g (1¹/₂oz) each flower paste and bought marine
　　blue sugarpaste

EQUIPMENT

30 x 25cm (12 x 10 in) oval cake board
templates (see pages 38 and 91)
scriber
scalpel
No. 00 paintbrush
Dresden tool
small holly cutter
small ivy leaf cutter
parchment piping bags and No. 1 piping tube (tip)
anglepoise lamp
Garrett frill cutter
1m (1yd) dark blue ribbon for cake
1m (1yd) gold ribbon for cake board

1　　Cover the cake with marzipan. Colour the marine blue sugarpaste with blueberry paste colouring to create a more intense midnight blue. Use to cover the cake and board; leave to dry. Attach the cake to the board with a little royal icing.

2　　Make two templates. Position one on the top of the cake and scribe the design onto the sugarpaste. Use the other as a template for all the cut-outs. Colour small pieces of flower paste using the picture as a guide, roll and cut out the shapes, starting at the furthest point and gradually working forwards. Fix in position with gum arabic as you work. Leave to dry. Paint in the creases and folds of the clothes, features, etc, and the hay in the foreground.

Actual size

3   To make the doorway, colour a large grape-size piece of flower paste with chestnut and dark brown paste colourings. Roll out fairly thickly, in two sections if preferred. Indent the inner edge with the Dresden tool. Fix in position with gum arabic and leave to dry. Paint on the wood grain with dark brown paste colouring.

4   Dust around the halos with lemon dusting powder. Darken the area inside the stable and around the edge of the large halo with dark warm brown dusting powder. Dust the area outside the door with navy dusting powder.

5   Colour a large grape-size piece of flower paste with emerald green dusting powder, mint green paste colouring and a touch of black paste colouring. Roll out thinly and cut out small leaves with the holly cutter. Soften the cut edges and indent a vein with the Dresden tool. Colour a large grape-size piece of paste pale cream. Roll out thinly and cut out small leaves with the ivy leaf cutter. Soften and vein as above, then paint the centre with spruce green paste colouring.

6   Colour 30g (1oz) royal icing with mint green, cream and a touch of black paste colourings and pipe the fern onto the cake with the No. 1 tube. Colour a little icing with strong red powder and pipe on the berries.

7   Use run-out icing (see page 8) and the templates to make 20 robins, strong red for the breast and chestnut for the brown area. Dry under the lamp. Attach the holly, ivy and robins to the doorway to form the garland, as shown.

8   To make the Garrett frill, knead the flower paste and sugar paste together well. Add a little more blueberry paste colouring to match the cake. Cut the frill and attach to the cake with gum arabic. Make leaves, berries and robins as above and attach to the upper edge of the frill, as shown. Pipe on fern as above.

9   Colour the royal icing with blueberry paste colouring to match the cake. Use to pipe a snail's trail around the base of the cake. Leave to dry, then attach the dark blue ribbon. Fix the gold ribbon around the cake board.

Candle Cake

This small cake would make an ideal present for someone on their own at Christmas. The twigs, Christmas roses and foliage around the base of the candle could be replaced with marzipan fruits if time – or skill – is short.

CAKE AND DECORATIONS

500g (1lb) marzipan (almond paste)
cake baked in deep narrow round tin (see Note)
boiled, sieved apricot jam (jelly)
625g (1¼lb) white sugarpaste
185g (6oz) flower paste
black, yellow, tangerine, blueberry, brown, gooseberry, Christmas and spruce green, red, poinsettia and ruby paste colourings
60g (2oz) royal icing
moss, forest and apple green, lemon, pink and black dusting powders (petal dusts)
cornflour (cornstarch) for dusting
strong red powder colour
confectioners' glaze

EQUIPMENT

large and small ball tools
23cm (9 in) round cake board
5cm (2 in) piece dried spaghetti
brown, green and white stem-wrap
brown 26-gauge wires
tweezers
small, medium and large blossom cutters
40-50 yellow stamens
green 30-gauge wires
Christmas rose petal cutter
white 24- and 28-gauge wires
poinsettia, Christmas rose, holly and birdfoot ivy leaf veiners
small pieces of foam
birdfoot ivy and holly leaf cutters
small rose petal cutter
scalpel
No. 1 paintbrush
1m (1yd) green ribbon for bows
1m (1yd) red ribbon for cake board

1　Roll out the marzipan to a rectangle large enough to enclose the cake. Lay the cake on the marzipan and trim the marzipan to the same length. Brush the cake with jam. Roll the cake, wrapping it in the marzipan until it is completely covered. Trim away excess marzipan. Stand the cake upright and work on the seam: butt the edges together and smooth over the join using the warmth of the hand until the seam line is invisible.

2　Cut out a circle of marzipan for the top of the cake and attach, keeping the edge sharp. Form a slight hollow in the centre with the large ball tool. Roll the cake in sugarpaste as above to cover completely. Allow a little extra paste for the top of the candle, as shown. Gently pinch the upper edge to form melted wax, as shown. Keep the outer surface smooth and straight at the top of the candle where the paste has been pinched. Cover the cake board with white sugarpaste; leave to dry. Attach the candle to the centre of the board with a little royal icing.

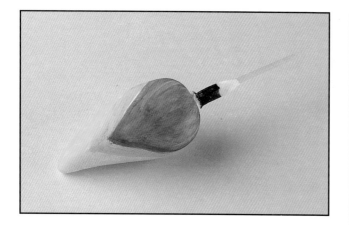

CANDLE FLAME

3 Roll a grape-size piece of white sugarpaste into a cone and curve the top to create a flickering effect. Place the piece of spaghetti into the base of the cone. Roll a small sausage of white flower paste and push onto the spaghetti, butting it against the base of the flame. Leave to dry, then paint black. Paint the flame yellow, orange and blue, as shown. Insert into the hollowed-out area at the top of the cake.

TWIGS

4 Fold a length of brown stem-wrap and cut into three strips. Twist the end of one strip and fold to form a small nob. Attach to the brown 26-gauge wire. Work halfway down the wire. Snap off the stem-wrap. Create another bud on the opposite side of the wire. Work down the wire in this manner. Bend the twig with tweezers at each bud to create a natural effect. Prepare several twigs in this way.

LARCH CONES

5 Colour 60g (2oz) flower paste light brown. Cut a piece of brown 26-gauge wire 7.5cm (3 in) long. Attach a pip-size ball of paste to the hooked end and leave to dry overnight. Cut three blossoms using the large cutter. Soften and cup the petals with the small ball tool. Draw up each petal towards the centre of the blossom but *do not* thin the edges. Pull the wire with the dried ball attached through the centre of the blossom and cover completely. Repeat the process for the next two shapes but leave slightly more open. Cut out two medium and two small blossoms and one more large blossom. Place a small piece of flower paste between each of the last five blossom shapes so that when they are attached to the wire each layer remains separate to give a more open and rounded egg-like shape. Cut and twist green stem-wrap to form thin needles, as shown. Gently bend the wire of the larch cone to form a gentle curve. Attach to the twig with needles as shown.

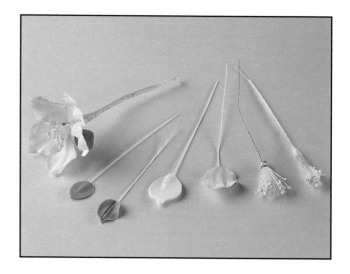

CHRISTMAS ROSES

6 Wire together 40 to 50 flat-headed yellow stamens, then splay out. Dust the stamen cotton light green with moss dusting powder. Strengthen the main stem with a white 24-gauge wire then cover with white stem-wrap.

7 PETALS: Roll out white flower paste, slightly thicker than is usual for flowers, as a Christmas rose is quite fleshy. Roll the paste so that the base of the petal will be thicker than the top. Leave a slight ridge down the centre in which to insert a white 28-gauge wire. Cut out the petal, insert the wire then vein. Soften the edge of the petal with the ball tool. Place the petal on a pre-formed piece of foam to curve slightly and leave to dry.

8 Colour a grape-size piece of flower paste goose-berry green. Roll out and use the rose petal cutter to make two small leaves. Leave a central ridge in which to place a white 28-gauge wire, ball the edge, twist to give movement and leave to dry.

9 Colour the base of the Christmas rose petal in an upwards movement with a mixture of moss green and lemon dusting powders made lighter by mixing with cornflour. Dust the edge of the petals and one edge of the green leaves with pink. Wire the petals around the stamens, then place the leaves underneath the flower. Thicken the stem of the flower with white stem-wrap and dust with a mix of green and pink.

IVY LEAVES

10 Colour about 30g (1oz) flower paste Christmas green. Roll out thinly but leave a ridge in the centre of the leaf in which to place a green 28-gauge wire. Cut out the leaf using the birdfoot ivy leaf cutter, then vein. Ball the edges to give movement. Leave to dry. Paint the area between the veins, as shown, with varying tones of Christmas green: use the colour as a wash for the paler tones and a little thicker for the deeper tone. Dust all the edges with a mixture of forest green and a touch of black. Dust one edge slightly darker (add more black). Flash the leaf over a steaming kettle to add a sheen and fix the dusting powders. Make an assortment of leaf sizes. When wiring together, place the smallest leaf at the top of the spray and gradually add slightly larger leaves, bending the stems to give movement, as shown.

HOLLY AND BERRIES

11 Colour a large grape-size piece of flower paste with strong red powder colour for the berries. Roll into a small oval then draw in a 28-gauge wire with a very small hook. Pinch the top of the berry with tweezers to form a rough raised shape as shown. Leave to dry. Paint the raised area black and glaze the rest of the berry with confectioners' glaze.

12 Colour a plum-size piece of flower paste with Christmas green, a touch of brown and a touch of black. Colour a similar size piece of paste with a lighter tone of Christmas green. To make the holly leaves, take two large pea-size pieces of each colour, roll into individual balls, then press together. Roll out the paste, leaving a ridge in the centre, and cut out. Insert a 26-gauge wire, then vein. Ball the edges firmly between the points to give plenty of movement. Twist the leaf, support on foam and leave to dry. Dust the edge with dark forest green and black. Steam (see step 10). Wire together in groups of five leaves with three to five berries, as shown.

POINSETTIA

13 If possible, work from an actual poinsettia to create a more natural flower. Colour a pea-size piece of flower paste a light Christmas green. Take a small pip-size piece and form a cone. Pull a hooked 30-gauge wire into the paste, make two small cuts in the top of the cone and fold back. Create a depression between the cuts with the scalpel. Leave to dry, then paint this top area red. Paint small leaf shapes around the bud. Create several buds, some small and some large. Colour 30g

(1oz) flower paste with strong red powder colour. Roll out the paste thinly, leaving a ridge in the centre of the bract in which to insert the wire. Use a 28-gauge wire for the small bracts and a 26-gauge wire for the larger outer bracts. Vein with the poinsettia veiner. Cut around the edge of the bract and soften with a ball tool to give movement. Support on foam and leave to dry. Make two or three small bracts, four or five slightly larger, four or five medium and three large.

14 Colour 15g (¹⁄₂oz) flower paste with gooseberry green paste colouring (for the patterned leaves) and 15g (¹⁄₂oz) a darker green with Christmas green, a touch of blueberry and a touch of black. Make all the leaves using the largest veiner. Make just a few pale green leaves and about five darker leaves for the patterned leaves. When dry, paint on dark green veins with a fine brush and spruce green paste colouring. Paint the red areas between the veins with poinsettia and ruby paste colourings. Leave to dry. Dust the areas around the central vein with a mix of forest and apple green and black dusting powders, as shown. Dust the edges of the leaf red on one side and the black/green mix on the other. On the darker leaves, paint the veins with the poinsettia colour. Dust the edges of the leaves with red, then black/green on one side edge.

15 Wire the buds tightly together. Shred white stem-wrap into thin strips and use to wrap the stems of the bracts. Dust red. Bend the wire at a 90° angle, 1cm (¹⁄₂ in) from the base of the bract. Attach the smallest bract to the main stem under the buds. Continue to add the bracts, gradually increasing the size, as shown. Dust the stems of the leaves red/green and add to the base of the flower.

TO COMPLETE

16 Roll a large sausage of sugarpaste into a 2.5cm (1 in) wide coil and wrap around the base of the candle. Insert the finished flowers and leaves (see main picture), taking care not to insert any wires directly into the cake. Finish with green bows. Fix the ribbon around the cake board.

NOTE: A deep narrow round tin (can) is best for this cake, e.g. a hot dog or asparagus tin. Line it with Eezi-off so that the cake can be easily removed. Depending on the tin used, you will need approximately half the quantity of cake mix used for a 20cm (8 in) round cake.

Larch needles could be made more quickly by winding some green sylko cotton around the fingers approximately twenty times. Place a piece of fine wire through one end of the cotton loop and bind tightly. Trim to size.

A Winter's Scene

This beautiful cake has a sunken gelatine plaque in the centre and an elaborate suparpaste collar with bas-relief robin and ivy.

CAKE AND DECORATIONS

19 x 21cm (7¹/₂ x 8¹/₂ in) rectangular cake
1.25kg (2¹/₂lb) marzipan (almond paste)
boiled, sieved apricot jam (jelly)
2kg (4lb) bought celebration colour sugarpaste
90g (3oz) royal icing
gelatine paste (see page 8)
brown, dark brown, chestnut, dark cream, Christmas green, red and black paste colourings
brown, cream, forest green, black, dark red and white dusting powders (petal dusts)
75g (2¹/₂oz) flower paste
1¹/₂ tsp gum tragacanth
90g (3oz) modelling paste
gum arabic (see page 8)
extra albumen powder (optional)

EQUIPMENT

smoother
30cm (12 in) square cake board
absorbent kitchen paper
templates (see pages 86 and 87)
plaque cutter
lip pencil
Nos. 00 and 1 paintbrushes
ivy leaf cutters
16 pieces of 33-gauge wire
beige stem-wrap
scalpel
small ball tool
Dresden tool
ivy veiners – various sizes
parchment piping bags and No. 3 piping tube (tip)
anglepoise lamp
cotton bud
1.5m (1¹/₂yd) dark green ribbon for cake board

1   Cut out an 11 x 18cm (4¹/₂ x 7 in) section 1cm (¹/₂ in) deep from the centre of the cake. Use a sharp kitchen knife and keep the sides and corners of the cavity as straight and sharply angled as possible, as the square will diminish in size and the corners and edges become rounded when covered with marzipan and sugarpaste.

2   Roll out the marzipan and use to cover the cake. Drape it over the cake, make a slit in the centre and gently ease it into the cavity. Use a smoother to ensure all the edges and corners are as flat and sharp as possible. It does not matter if the base is not completely covered as it will be covered with a plaque. Repeat with the sugarpaste and leave to dry. Cover the cake board with sugarpaste and leave to dry. Attach the cake to the board with a little royal icing.

PLAQUE

3   Make a template of the base of the hollow with absorbent kitchen paper so that you can get right into the corners. Using the template and plaque cutter make a gelatine plaque. Leave to dry.

4   Using the plaque template and sharp lip pencil, draw the winter's scene lightly on the gelatine plaque. Carefully paint on the scene using a fairly dry brush (too much water will melt the paste) and paste colourings. Soften the image by using dusting powders to create sky, shadows in snow, etc. Leave to dry completely. Apply some royal icing to the base of the hollow and place the plaque in position.

5   Colour the flower paste with Christmas green paste colouring and use to make some tiny ivy leaves on 33-gauge wire, using the template as a pattern. Wrap beige stem-wrap around two wires and twist together. Repeat with two more wires. Join together, forming loops, twists and bumps to create a natural effect. Place on the plaque, bending at each corner. Wire the leaves together and attach to the twisted wire as shown.

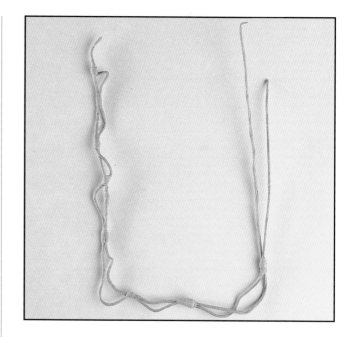

COLLAR

6   Trace the collar template onto good quality tracing paper or fine card. Remove the shaded areas with the scalpel. Knead the gum tragacanth into 750g (1½lb) sugarpaste and leave to dry for 24 hours.

7   Roll out the sugarpaste to 7.5mm (³/₈ in) thick. Position the template and carefully cut out the collar, removing the inner shapes. If preferred, cut the collar into two sections so that it is less likely to break when handling, as the filigree effect will weaken the collar. Leave to dry thoroughly, then attach to the top of the cake with cream royal icing.

8   Repeat the twisted wire effect around the base of the cake and attach more ivy leaves, as shown. Make the leaves on the right and left hand sides bigger to echo the shape and size of the leaves on the collar.

ROBINS

9 Work on the background shapes first, gradually working forwards to give a 3D effect. Use the tracing as a template for the various shapes. Colour the modelling paste with brown, dark brown and chestnut. Roll out some of the paste quite thinly, cut out the tail and attach to the collar with gum arabic. Mark on the feathers with the scalpel. Trim away any excess paste.

10 Roll out some sugarpaste 5mm (¼ in) thick. Cut out the entire body. Smooth the edges and round with fingers. Attach to the collar with gum arabic. Mark in the eye with the small ball tool. Mark the indentations on the chest etc. with the Dresden tool. When the varying shapes of the body have been clearly defined, mark on the feathers with the scalpel.

11 Cut out the wing and head in brown modelling paste and attach to the body with gum arabic. Mark as before with the Dresden tool and scalpel. Colour a small piece of modelling paste dark cream, cut out and attach a beak with gum arabic.

TWIGS

12 Roll the same brown modelling paste into a thin rope, twist and pinch into shape. Attach to the collar with gum arabic. Indent with the Dresden tool so that the twigs look gnarled and twisted.

IVY LEAVES

13 Using the Christmas green flower paste and the tracing as a template, cut out the leaves, vein, then soften the edges with the small ball tool. Twist the leaves to create a natural effect. Place on the collar to check they fit correctly, *but do not attach at this stage*. Leave to dry.

14 Paint the area between the veins with varying tones of Christmas green. Use the colour as a wash for the paler tone and a little thicker for the deeper tone. Dust all the edges with a mixture of forest green and a touch of black. Dust one side with a darker green (add more black). Flash the leaf over a steaming kettle to add a sheen and fix the dusting powders.

TO FINISH

15 Thin the royal icing to run-out consistency (see page 8) and colour pale cream to match the collar. Pipe over the area that will still be visible, i.e. between the leaves, the outer edges of the collar, on top of the wings, etc., with the No. 3 piping tube. When applying the icing to the outer edge of the left and right sides, dry each small area under the lamp before applying the next, to create the snow-like effect.

16 Paint the breasts of the robins with a mixture of red and a touch of black paste colourings. Remove some of the colour in places with the cotton bud so that the overall effect appears to be more 3D. Leave to dry, then dust with dark red, a touch of black and white. Dust the brown area under the wing, tail, etc. with a darker brown. Pipe a small bulb of black royal icing into the eye socket, leave to dry, then paint with the No. 1 brush and gum arabic to glaze. Pipe on pale brown feet.

17 Attach the leaves with a small bulb of cream royal icing. Fix the ribbon around the cake board.

Christmas Bauble

This beautiful, very unusual cake is one for the more experienced cake decorator.
The technique used is bas relief.

CAKE AND DECORATIONS
20cm (8 in) round cake
1.35kg (2³/₄lb) marzipan (almond paste)
boiled, sieved apricot jam (jelly)
1.5kg (3lb) bought red sugarpaste
60g (2oz) bought marine blue sugarpaste
blueberry, melon, dark brown, tartrazine-free cream,
    red and Christmas green paste colourings
60g (2oz) white sugarpaste
gum arabic (see page 8)
250g (8oz) modelling paste
navy, light blue, brown and grey dusting powders
    (petal dusts)
90g (3oz) royal icing
extra albumen powder (optional)
cornflour (cornstarch) for dusting
silver food colouring

EQUIPMENT
soccer ball cake tin
15cm (6 in) round plaque cutter
smoother
23cm (11 in) round cake board
template (see page 50)
Nos. 0, 1 and 2 paintbrushes
small ball tool
parchment piping bags and Nos. 1 and 2 piping tubes
    (tips)
candle holder (for moulding bauble cap)
3.5cm (1¹/₂ in) round biscuit (cookie) cutter
1m (1yd) red-gold ribbon

1   Make and bake the cake using a soccer ball cake tin. If the cake rises in the middle, cut away the excess so that when the two halves are placed together a neat join is formed. Soften some marzipan with a little of the warmed jam and use to sandwich the two cake halves together. Make a long thin sausage of marzipan and push between the join to hide any imperfections and gaps, as shown. Push the plaque cutter 2.5cm (1 in) into the upper half of the cake. Cut around the inner edge of the cutter with a sharp knife. Cut across the circle, forming a cross. Remove the cut area in sections. Using a dessertspoon, carve out the hollow until the shape of a half grapefruit has been achieved, as shown. Strengthen any broken areas on the rim of the hollow with marzipan.

2   Measure the circumference of the ball. Roll out the marzipan to a round large enough to cover the ball. Brush the warmed jam over the cake. Place the cake on the marzipan and lift the marzipan gently upwards towards the hollowed-out section. Trim away any excess. Smooth all creases firmly with the smoother and warmth of the hand. Use the plaque cutter to cut the opening of

the hollow again, to create a clean, sharp edge. *Do not cover the inside of hollow at this stage.* Place the cake at an angle and leave to dry.

3　Roll out the marzipan quite thinly to the size of a small tea-plate and place inside the hollow. Smooth with the underside of the spoon, trim the edge with a sharp knife then smooth the cut edge with fingers to round. Leave to dry.

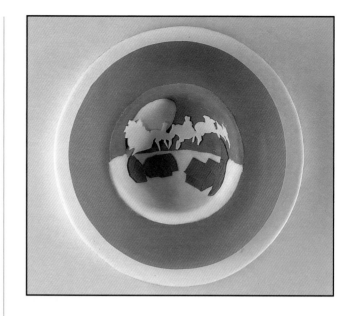

4　Cover the cake with red sugarpaste in the same way, leaving the inside of the hollow uncovered. Attach to the cake board at an angle with a little royal icing. Colour the marine blue sugarpaste with blueberry paste colouring to a deep midnight blue and roll out as thinly as possible. Using the template, cut out the shape of the sky. Moisten the inside of the hollow and insert the 'sky'.

Enlarge by 125% on a photocopier

5 Using the template and white sugarpaste as before, cut out and attach the snow shape. Smooth the join between sky and snow with a finger until it becomes less obvious. Trim the edge of the hollow with a sharp knife and smooth as before.

6 Colour 22g (³/₄oz) sugarpaste with a touch of melon. Roll into a ball, then flatten between the palms to give a slightly domed effect for the moon. Fix in place with gum arabic.

7 Colour 30g (1oz) modelling paste with dark brown and cream paste colourings until a yellow/brown colour has been achieved. Roll out and cut out the shapes of the houses as shown. For any shapes standing proud, eg. porches, end walls, chimneys, cut a further shape and attach to the main shape. Fix in place with gum arabic.

8 Trace the outline and main details only of Father Christmas and the reindeer. Roll out a small piece of white modelling paste and cut around the template. Attach over the moon and curve across the sky. Leave to dry.

9 Paint in the window panes, doors, reindeer with antlers, sleigh and Father Christmas using the No. 0 brush. Add walls and gates to front gardens to separate and produce a more natural effect. Paint some Christmas green trees onto the background surrounding the houses then, using a dry brush, stipple on a little Christmas green mixed with dark brown to give shadowed effects. Dust the sky with navy dusting powder and the snow in the foreground with a little light blue. Dust Father Christmas and the reindeer with brown/grey to soften the colour. Pipe dots of white royal icing with the No. 1 tube to represent snowflakes.

10 Roll a plum-size piece of white modelling paste into a ball. Place on the bottom edge of the bauble, pinch the edges to form the roof shape and indent a square hole to accommodate a chimney. Make a brick shape with the brown paste, hollow out the top but keep the square shape. Insert into the hole and fix with a little gum arabic. Use a tiny ball tool to indent small footprints.

11 Make a 1.5cm (¾ in) high cone with a large grape-size piece of Christmas green modelling paste. Cut small Vs into the cone and press into the house at the base of the bauble. Leave to dry. Thin some royal icing to run-out consistency (see page 8) and pipe onto these branches and the background trees with the No. 1 tube.

12 Roll a large plum-size piece of white modelling paste into a long thin sausage. Attach around the edge of the hollow, flatten and smooth with fingers. Paint silver with the No. 2 brush.

13 To make the metal cap for the top of the bauble, form 125g (4oz) white modelling paste into a thick roll and open up one end with the thumbs. Dust the candle holder liberally with cornflour. Place the paste inside the candle holder, pressing against it with the fingers and removing periodically to check on the shape being formed. When satisfied, remove from the mould and cut away the excess paste. Rest it on the cake to dry so that

it fits snugly. To make a ring for the cap, roll out 30g (1oz) modelling paste as thinly as possible. Cut a long strip 5mm (¼ in) wide with a sharp knife. Wrap around the biscuit cutter. Butt the ends together and fold back 1cm (½ in). Cut away the excess and leave to dry. Attach to the cap with royal icing. Paint the cap and ring with silver food colouring using the No. 2 brush and leave to dry. Attach the cap to the cake with royal icing. Loop the ribbon through the ring, drape over the cake and attach with a little royal icing.

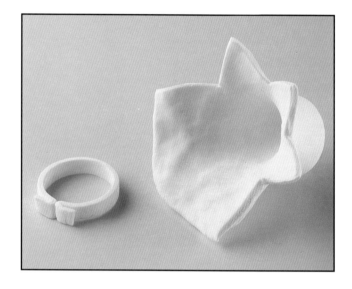

NOTE: Remove the silver cap and ring before eating the cake – silver colouring is not edible.

Pastoral Peace

A painted gelatine plaque inserted in the centre of the cake and surrounded by Christmas foliage creates a beautiful, pastoral scene. Techniques used include brush embroidery, cut-out and run-out.

CAKE AND DECORATIONS

gelatine paste (see page 8)
20cm (8 in) round cake
boiled, sieved apricot jam (jelly)
1.25kg (2½lb) marzipan (almond paste)
1.25kg (2½lb) sugarpaste
60g (2oz) royal icing
tartrazine-free cream, chestnut, dark brown,
*   gooseberry, spruce and Christmas green and*
*   black paste colourings*
60g (2oz) modelling paste
1 tsp piping gel
30g (1oz) flower paste
gum arabic (see page 8)
grey, green and lilac dusting powders (petal dusts)
strong red powder colour

EQUIPMENT

10cm (4 in) round plaque cutter
23cm (11 in) round cake board
parchment piping bags and Nos. 1 and 2 piping tubes
*   (tips)*
template (see page 95)
scriber
Nos. 1 and 2 paintbrushes
cel pad
ball tool
small pieces of foam
holly and Christmas rose veiners
cocktail stick (toothpick)
yellow stamens
tweezers
1m (1yd) thin red ribbon for cake base
1m (1yd) green ribbon for cake board

1   Make a gelatine plaque using the gelatine paste and plaque cutter. Leave to dry.

2   Cover the cake with marzipan and sugarpaste. Using the plaque cutter, remove a 10cm (4 in) circle from the centre while still soft. Cover the cake board with sugarpaste; leave to dry. Attach the cake to the board with a little royal icing. Pipe a snail's trail around the base of the cake with the No. 1 piping tube.

3   Using the template, scribe the church onto the plaque, then paint with paste colours. (For technique see Christmas Garland, page 22.) Apply a little royal icing to the base of the hollow and place the plaque in position. Pipe small dots over the scene with the No. 1 piping tube to represent snow.

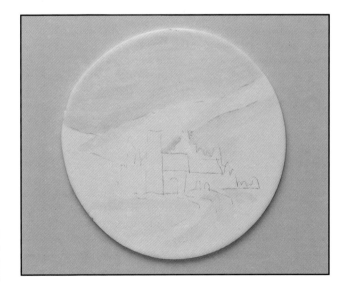

4   Using the template, scribe the main design onto the top of the cake around the inset. Roll out the modelling paste thinly. Trace the overlapping base template, place on the paste and carefully cut around the shape. Leave to dry thoroughly. Place on the cake, matching the design, and attach with royal icing.

icing into place. Outline the Christmas rose bud using the No. 2 piping tube, then brush the icing downwards to the base of the bud (see Noel, Noel, page 76). Colour a little of the icing with a touch of spruce green and black to give a grey/green colour and pipe the calyx at the base of the bud in the same way.

7 Roll out the flower paste so that it will be thicker at the base of the petal. Using the template, cut out the Christmas rose, then vein. Thin the cut edge with the ball tool. Curl some of the edges with the cocktail stick to give a natural effect. Leave to dry. Working from the back forwards, attach the holly leaves and Christmas roses to the cake with gum arabic.

8 Colour a very small amount of royal icing with the merest touch of cream and gooseberry green to make a yellow/lime colour. Pipe a small bulb in the middle of each flower. Curve some fine yellow stamens by dragging a thumbnail along the cotton. Place in the bulb of icing with tweezers, as shown. Dust the background around the flowers and leaves with grey/green and grey/lilac.

9 To make the holly berries, colour a grape-size piece of modelling paste with strong red powder colour. Roll into small balls and attach to the cake with royal icing. Paint on a black dot. Fix the ribbons around the cake base and board to finish.

5 Starting at the back and working forwards, paint on the light leaves. For the holly leaves in the foreground, colour a large grape-size piece of modelling paste with Christmas green, a little dark brown and a touch of black paste colourings. Using the template, cut out the leaves, vein, then place on the cel pad. Curve between the points of the holly with the ball tool and twist to give movement. Place the leaves in position, support with small pieces of foam if necessary and leave to dry.

6 Stir the piping gel into the royal icing: this will slow the setting time and create more time to brush the

Madonna and Child

Cocoa painting is used to create this peaceful design.
Similar in technique to painting with oils, it can be a quick and easy
way to decorate a cake. The finished effect resembles early sepia photographs.

CAKE AND DECORATIONS
15 x 20cm (6 x 8in) oval cake
boiled, sieved apricot jam (jelly)
1kg (2lb) marzipan (almond paste)
1kg (2lb) bought celebration colour sugarpaste
60g (2oz) royal icing
cocoa butter (see Note)
cocoa powder
blueberry paste colouring

EQUIPMENT
25 x 30cm (10 x 12in) oval cake board
templates (see below and page 58)
scriber
4 small screw-top jars
Nos. 2, 1 and 0 paintbrushes
parchment piping bags and No. 1 piping tube (tip)
1m (1yd) each light and dark brown thin ribbon for
    base of cake
1m (1yd) dark brown ribbon for cake board

Enlarge by 114%
on a photocopier

1 Marzipan the cake, then cover the cake and board with sugarpaste; leave to dry. Attach the cake to the board with a little royal icing. Scribe the template onto the cake or trace the outline with a sharp pencil. Do not put in too much detail as the lines could show through the lighter tones of the cocoa butter and spoil the finished image.

2 Put small amounts of cocoa butter in the jars and put in a shallow pan of hot water to melt. Add a little cocoa powder to the first jar, a little more to the second and even more to the third to give three distinct tones. In the fourth jar, make quite a concentrated mix for defining the features and any deep shadows in the folds of the clothing.

3 Cover the baby and Madonna in the palest tone, as shown. While still warm, add the second tone to the faces, hands and part of the blanket and clothing. Add the third tone (see left hand picture page 58). Add the darkest

tones to the eyelashes, pupils, nostrils, fingers, hair and deepest areas of clothing. Add a little blueberry paste colouring to the lightest tone and brush over the lighter areas of the Madonna's veil and dress. Leave to dry. Create highlights in the hair, eyes, etc. with the scriber or a scalpel.

Actual size

4   Paint on the town of Bethlehem using the same technique. Pipe a small snail's trail around the base of the cake with white royal icing and the No. 1 tube. Leave to dry, then attach the ribbons above the piping, forming bows as shown. Fix the ribbon around the cake board to finish.

NOTE: Cocoa butter can be difficult to obtain and quite expensive. Coconut oil, available from good food stores or healthfood shops, makes a good substitute. Keep the jars in the water and keep the water hot while working. Any unused cocoa butter can be stored; to re-use, put the jars in hot water and stir the butter thoroughly.

Festive Robins

To give added support to this intricate open collar,
the shape of the collar is first flooded with icing to form a base.
The design is then traced and flooded directly onto that.

CAKE AND DECORATIONS

20cm (8 in) round cake
boiled, sieved apricot jam (jelly)
1.25kg (2½lb) marzipan (almond paste)
1.5kg (3lb) royal icing
extra albumen powder (optional)
skintone, apricot, cream, nutkin, lemon yellow, moss
*   and forest green, cornflower blue and brown*
*   dusting powders (petal dusts)*
strong red and strong black powder colours
black and forest green paste colourings

EQUIPMENT

28cm (11 in) round cake board
straight edge and side scraper
templates (see pages 90 and 91)
30cm (12 in) square piece of perspex or glass
double-sided tape or spray glue
waxed paper or run-out film
parchment piping bags and No. 1 piping tube (tip)
anglepoise lamp
No. 1 paintbrush
cranked palette knife
1m (1yd) green ribbon for cake board

1 Marzipan the cake, then cover the cake and board with royal icing; leave to dry. Attach the cake to the board with a little royal icing.

2 Attach the top collar template to perspex or glass with double-sided tape or spray glue. Cover with waxed paper or run-out film, making sure there are no creases, and secure as above. Using the No. 1 piping tube and royal icing, outline the outer and inner edges of the design. Thin the remaining royal icing with water or dissolved albumen (see page 8) and flood the area between the piped outline, working from side to side so that the icing does not dry and form a line. Make a cut in the centre of the waxed paper to ease the tension and allow the collar to dry without cracking. Dry thoroughly under the lamp.

3 Make a second tracing of the template, then retrace the design on the back of the tracing paper. Place on the collar and *very carefully* redraw over the tracing. The design should now appear lightly on the collar. (If confident, the design can be drawn freehand as the main shapes will be apparent from the outline on the piped collar.)

4 Colour small amounts of the thinned royal icing with dusting powders as follows for the various shapes:

Chinese lantern – skintone and apricot
Medium leaves – cream and nutkin
Yellow-green smaller leaves – lemon yellow, moss green and apricot
Fern – moss green and cornflower blue
Holly – moss and forest green
Chestnuts – nutkin and moss green
Twigs and robin – nutkin and brown

Berries and robin's breast – strong red powder, left to darken for a few minutes before use
Robin's eyes – strong black powder, used as above.

5 Working from the back of the design forwards, flood the design onto the collar using piping bags and the No. 1 tube. Dry the icing periodically under the lamp as you work, to ensure it dries with a sheen. Leave to dry completely. Paint in detail dots on berries, veins, etc. with paste colourings and a fairly dry brush.

6 Draw and flood the base collar design directly onto the board in the same way. (There is no need to make the collar in white icing first.)

7 Very carefully remove the top collar from the waxed paper with the cranked palette knife. Attach to the top of the cake with dots of royal icing, making sure that the Chinese lanterns, chestnuts and large leaves correspond to the design on the board. Fix the ribbon around the cake board.

NOTE: The best way to flood small areas is to use a No. 1 piping tube. As long as the icing is the correct consistency, there is no need to outline the shapes first.

Candlelight

A traditional royal-iced cake simply decorated with run-out candles and cut-out holly leaves.

CAKE AND DECORATIONS
20 x 15cm (8 x 6 in) oval cake
boiled, sieved apricot jam (jelly)
1kg (2lb) marzipan (almond paste)
1kg (2lb) sugarpaste
125g (4oz) royal icing
extra albumen powder (optional)
melon, black, tangerine, tartrazine-free cream and
        Christmas green paste colourings
60g (2oz) flower paste
strong red powder colour
gum arabic (see page 8)

EQUIPMENT
30 x 25cm (12 x 10 in) oval cake board
template (see page 87)
glass or perspex
double-sided tape or spray glue
waxed paper or run-out film
parchment piping bags and Nos. 1 and 2 piping
        tubes (tips)
anglepoise lamp
cranked palette knife
scriber
scalpel
cel pad
ball tool
black food pen
paintbrush
2m (2yd) thin peach ribbon for base of cake
1m (1yd) peach ribbon for cake board

1   Marzipan the cake then cover the cake and board with sugarpaste; leave to dry. Attach the cake to the board with a little royal icing.

2   Attach the template to the glass or perspex with double-sided tape or spray glue. Cover with waxed paper or run-out film, ensuring there are no creases, and secure as above. Outline the circle and candles with firm peak royal icing and the No. 1 tube. Set aside enough icing to outline Noel and pipe a snail's trail. Thin the rest with water or dissolved albumen (see page 8).

3   Colour three-quarters of the thinned icing with a touch of melon to give a warm pale yellow colour. Flood the area inside the circle and around the candles using the No. 1 tube. Dry under the lamp so that the icing dries with a slight sheen.

4   Flood the candles with a little white royal icing, starting from the back and working forwards, then pipe on the melted wax with the No. 2 tube. Leave to dry. Colour a little icing with black colouring and pipe the wicks of the candles using the No. 1 tube. Dry thoroughly. Colour a little icing an orange/yellow with melon and tangerine colourings and pipe the candle flame with the No. 1 tube. Dry each area under the lamp as you work. Leave to dry completely. Paint on the darker inner flame.

Remove the royal iced disc from the waxed paper with the cranked palette knife and attach to the cake with a little royal icing. Pipe small dots of white icing around the disc with the No. 1 tube.

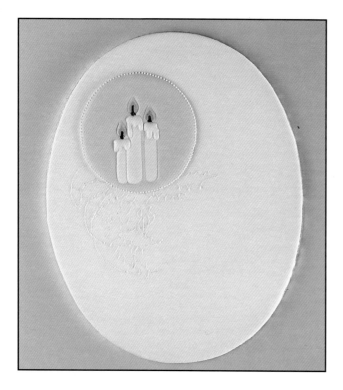

5   Make a second tracing of the leaves and twigs, position on the cake and impress the design with the scriber. Colour a little royal icing dark cream and pipe in the twigs with the No. 1 tube. Colour 45g (1½oz) flower paste a dark Christmas green and the remaining 15g (½oz) spruce green. Roll out thinly. Cut out leaf templates from the tracing and place on the dark green paste. Cut out carefully with the scalpel. Place on the cel pad and carefully soften the edges with the ball tool, ensuring that the points of the leaves are kept sharp. Twist to create shape and movement. Attach to the cake with royal icing, back leaves first. Cut out the underside of the leaves in the lighter green paste and attach as shown (see main picture).

6   Colour a little royal icing with the strong red powder colour and thin to a run-out consistency (see page 8). Pipe on the berries using the No. 2 tube. Dry under the lamp so that they dry with a sheen. Leave to dry completely, then draw on a black spot with the food pen. Glaze the leaves with gum arabic mixed with a touch of Christmas green paste colouring. Paint the glaze onto the leaves and leave to dry. Paint on the veins with a darker green.

7   Pipe around 'Noel' with reserved firm white icing and the No. 1 tube, then flood with run-out white icing and the same tube. Ease the icing into the corners with the paintbrush. Dry under the lamp. Pipe a snail's trail around the base of the cake with reserved firm white icing and the No. 1 tube. Attach two thin ribbons above it, forming a bow on one side as shown. Fix the ribbon around the cake board to finish.

Santa's Stocking

A fun cake for children, which can be as simple or as complicated as you choose.
The stocking itself is quite easy and will look good just on its own.
If you have a lot of time, toys of your children's choice –
made from modelling paste – will definitely add the finishing touch.
As a compromise, 'fill' the stocking with simple parcels.

CAKE AND DECORATIONS
20 x 30 x 5cm (8 x 12 x 2 in) slab cake
1.25kg (2½lb) marzipan (almond paste)
boiled, sieved apricot jam (jelly)
250g (8oz) white sugarpaste
1.5kg (3lb) bought red sugarpaste
30g (1oz) royal icing
gold food colouring
modelling paste and paste colourings for holly and
*   berries, toys or parcels*

EQUIPMENT
template (see page 93)
33 x 38cm (13 x 15 in) rectangular cake board
absorbent kitchen paper
new dishcloth
ribbed sports sock or cuff of cotton jumper
pastry wheel or scalpel
small ball tool
No. 1 paintbrush
holly leaf cutter
1.75m (1¾yd) red ribbon for cake board

1   Position the template on the cake and cut to shape. Round the top and bottom edges with a knife so that when the cake is covered the shape will appear to be rounded. Cut into the inner edge of the top of the stocking to create a curve.

2   Roll out the marzipan, bearing in mind the shape of the cake. Place the template on the marzipan. Leave 5cm (2 in) around the template to allow for covering the sides of the cake and cut the marzipan to shape. Cover the cake in the usual way, making sure the bottom edge turns under the cake. Create folds in the marzipan by indenting with fingers and thumbs. Exaggerate the indentations as they will become less evident when the cake is covered with sugarpaste. Cover the cake board with white sugarpaste and leave to dry.

3   Make a template of the stocking by laying a sheet of absorbent kitchen paper over the cake. Draw around the cake, omitting the heel and toe areas. Transfer this

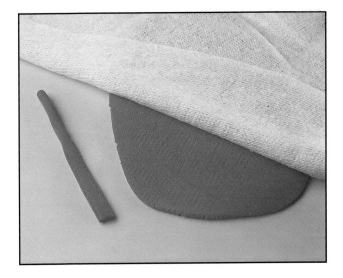

rough template onto good quality tracing paper. (The template on page 93 is a guide only, as the size will not be accurate.) Roll out the red sugarpaste. Place the new dishcloth on top and indent it into the paste by rolling over firmly once with a rolling pin to create a knitted texture. Place the template on the sugarpaste and cut out. Drape carefully over the marzipan and ease into place, taking care not to spoil the textured effect. Use kitchen paper to make a pattern for the heel and toe in the same way. Cut out in the textured paste and place in position on the cake, leaving a 5mm (1/4 in) gap between the heel and foot join.

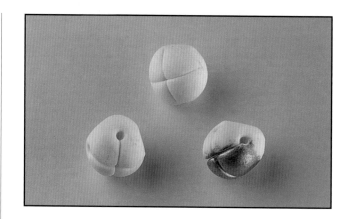

4　To make the ribbed toe section, cut the sock or jumper cuff vertically and open up to form a strip. Place on the red sugarpaste and texture as before. Cut and place the sugarpaste on the cake, leaving a 5mm (1/4 in) gap between the joins.

5　To fill the gaps between the shapes, roll a long thin section of red paste, flatten slightly and attach to the gaps. Make two lines of 'stitching' with the pastry wheel or tip of a scalpel. Leave the cake to dry, then attach to the board with a mixture of marzipan and apricot jam.

6　Lay absorbent kitchen paper over the top of the stocking and make a template for the zig-zag shape, allowing an extra 2.5cm (1 in) to roll over the top edge. Roll out all the red sugarpaste and texture with the dishcloth. Cut out, pinching the edges of the pointed shape with the cloth to eliminate the cut look. Attach to the stocking, taking care not to damage the textured effect. Roll over the top edge and turn in the corners.

Twist and curve the points to create an interesting and natural look. Leave to dry.

7　Roll six small grape-size pieces of white sugarpaste into balls for the bells. Make two cuts in the top of each with a kitchen knife. At each end of the cuts, indent a small hole with the ball tool. Indent a small hole at the top of the bell and insert the zig-zag points. Attach to the stocking with royal icing. Support the underneath of the bells on the board or cake with royal icing. Leave to dry, then paint gold.

8　Make some holly leaves and berries using modelling paste and place on the stocking. Make a selection of toys with modelling paste. Place 'inside' the top of the stocking, arranging so that some hang over the edge. Fix the ribbon around the cake board.

NOTE: Remove the bells from the cake before eating as gold colouring is not edible.

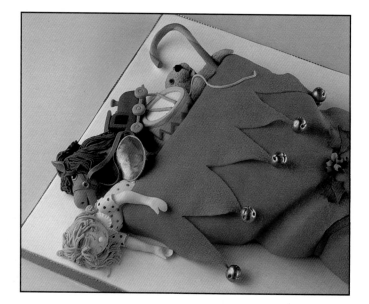

Mouse in a Flowerpot

An amusing novelty cake for those with a sense of humour.
A relatively simple cake to make with moulded figures and cut-out leaves.

CAKE AND DECORATIONS
20cm (8 in) round cake
boiled, sieved apricot jam (jelly)
1.25kg (2½lb) marzipan (almond paste)
1.25kg (2½lb) sugarpaste
185g (6oz) modelling paste
chestnut, tartrazine-free cream, brown and dark brown, black,
*   Christmas and gooseberry green paste colourings*
nutkin, brown and dark brown, cream, pink, black and
*   Christmas green dusting powders (petal dusts)*
gum arabic (see page 8)
strong red powder colour
125g (4oz) royal icing
60g (2oz) flower paste
gelatine crystals

GARRETT FRILL
30g (1oz) each sugarpaste and flower paste

EQUIPMENT
28cm (11 in) round cake board
5cm (2 in) plastic flowerpot
absorbent kitchen paper
waxed paper
sellotape and glue
an old No. 1 piping tube (tip)
large, medium and small ball tools
scriber
scalpel
Dresden tool
cocktail sticks (toothpicks)
templates (see pages 72 and 94)
fine tea-strainer
oak, holly and ivy leaf cutters
veiners for above
No. 1 paintbrush
26-, 28- and 33-gauge wire
black food pen
tweezers
brown stem-wrap
small polythene bag
parchment piping bags and No. 1 piping tube (tip)
Garrett frill cutter
1m (1yd) sandy ribbon for cake board

1   Marzipan the cake, then cover the cake and board with sugarpaste; leave to dry. Attach the cake to the board with a little royal icing.

FLOWERPOT
2   Colour 90g (3oz) modelling paste with chestnut, matching the depth of colour to the plastic flowerpot. Wrap a piece of absorbent kitchen paper around the flowerpot. Draw around the top and bottom edges of the pot and the rim to form an accurate template. (The templates on page 94 are a reference guide – they may not be an exact size.) Redraw the template on tracing paper so that the textured surface of the kitchen paper will not be transferred to the modelling paste when cutting out.

3   Cut out the template in waxed paper and sellotape it around the lower half of the pot. Roll out the chestnut modelling paste, cut out the shape using the traced template and wrap around the pot. Butt the cut ends together and stick with a little gum arabic. Make and wrap around the rim in the same way. Remove small sections from the top edge to form cracks and mark in the lines with a kitchen knife. Leave to dry completely, then carefully remove the plastic flowerpot. Using the template cut out the base of the pot in chestnut modelling paste and remove the central hole with the base of an old piping tube. Leave to dry. Attach to the bottom of the moulded pot with sticky 'glue' (see page 21). Smooth the base.

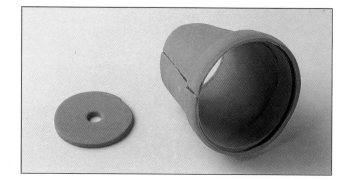

MOUSE

4   Colour 30g (1oz) modelling paste with nutkin, brown and cream dusting powders.
HEAD: Form a ball then a cone, indent with a small ball tool each side of the cone for the eyes. Use the scalpel to cut an upside-down Y for the mouth. Roll a tiny piece of pink paste (see below) into a ball and attach with gum arabic for the nose. Prick the base and insert the scriber at each side to form nostrils.

5   EARS: Colour a small ball of modelling paste nutkin brown and a smaller ball pale pink with dusting powders. Flatten, then place the pink ball in the centre of the brown. Pinch the ear together at the base and cut away the excess at the back. Insert the Dresden tool into the head to create an earhole and attach the ear with gum arabic. Texture the surface of the head with the scalpel to represent fur.

6   BODY: Form a cone with a grape-size piece of the coloured modelling paste. Cut away the base of the cone to form a curve for the base of the back. Place in the flowerpot to check the curve. Make an indentation with the small ball tool at the top of the cone in which to place the arms, a larger indentation at the base of the cone for the legs, and a hole with a cocktail stick at the very bottom of the cone for the tail. Roll a fine strand of pale pink paste, insert in the hole and drape naturally for the tail. Texture as above.

7   ARMS AND LEGS: Roll an elongated cone and bend for the elbow. Fix in position with gum arabic and fold across the stomach. Repeat for the other arm. Form

a similar but larger cone for the leg. Make two bends and attach as shown. Leave to dry. To make hands and feet, roll a pip-size piece of pink paste into a short sausage. Flatten to form a spade shape, then cut four fingers or toes and roll each gently. Curl and attach to the arm or leg with gum arabic and smooth the join. Place a small nut between the paws (see step 20) and attach with gum arabic.

8   EYES: Colour a pip-size piece of modelling paste with black dusting powder. Roll into tiny balls and position for the eyes. Leave to dry, then glaze with gum arabic.

ROBIN

9   Roll a large grape-size piece of white modelling paste into a ball, then into a cone. Texture the surface with the Dresden tool and scalpel to create feathers. Upturn the tail and make a depression for the head with the large ball tool.

10   HEAD: Roll a tiny grape-size piece of paste into a ball and place on a cocktail stick. Indent the eyes and a hole for the beak with the small ball tool. Make black eyes as above (step 8). Colour a pip-size piece of paste yellow-brown with tartrazine-free cream and a touch of dark brown paste colourings for the beak. Form a ball then a cone. Cut in half with the scalpel, then open up and insert the pointed end of the Dresden tool. Push the beak against the thumb to open up. Texture the head as above (step 9). Leave to dry.

11   Colour a grape-size piece of modelling paste brown with chestnut and dark brown paste colourings. Cut out the tail using the template. Indent feather marks with a sharp kitchen knife and scalpel. Ball the outline to soften. Place over the lower body, shape and curve as shown. Leave to dry, then paint with brown paste colouring. Paint the breast red and the lower body around the tail brown.

12 COAT: Wrap the body in absorbent kitchen paper to make the pattern for the coat shape (use the template on page 72 as a guide). Transfer the shape onto tracing paper and cut out. Colour a small grape-size piece of modelling paste with strong red powder colour. Roll out thinly, place the template on top and cut out the coat. Attach to the body with gum arabic. Push some white modelling paste through the tea-strainer to create fur and attach to the coat. Pipe on white buttons.

13 Paint the robin's head as shown and attach to the body with royal icing.

14 HAT: Roll a small grape-size piece of red paste into a very long elongated cone. Insert the medium ball tool until the hat fits the robin's head. Bring the end down over the robin's eyes. Make and attach fur as above.

15 Colour a tiny piece of modelling paste grey using black paste colouring and form six fine threads for the front of the feet. Attach in place with royal icing. Place the robin on the cake and fix with gum arabic.

OAK LEAVES

16 Colour a pea-size piece of flower paste with tartrazine-free cream and chestnut paste colourings to create a yellow ochre colour. Roll out thinly and cut out oak leaves. Vein the leaves and ball the edges firmly to frill, then thin to create tears. Cut out extra tears and holes with the old piping tube and paint the edges with dark brown paste colouring. Leave to dry, then dust with black/brown dusting powders.

HOLLY

17 Colour a pea-size piece of flower paste Christmas green. Roll out the paste and cut out holly leaves; leave a thickened ridge down the centre of the leaf in which to insert a 28-gauge wire. Vein the leaves and ball the edges as above to soften, then twist to create a natural effect. Make berries with small balls of red paste. Insert a 33-gauge wire and leave to dry. Paint a black mark on the tip with the food pen. Dust the edges with black/green dusting powders and flash over a steaming kettle to create a sheen.

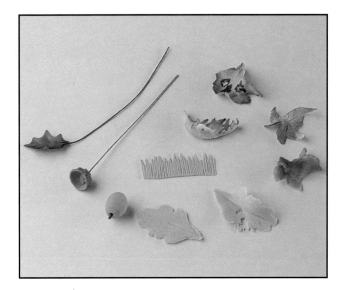

IVY

18 Colour a pea-size piece of flower paste with gooseberry green paste colouring. Cut, vein, ball and wire leaves as before.

NUTS

19 Colour a small pea-size piece of flower paste with tartrazine-free cream and chestnut paste colourings to achieve a warm golden brown. To create a natural effect, work from an actual cob nut and acorn if possible; if not, refer to a book.

20 COB NUTS: Roll a pea-size piece of paste into a ball. Pinch and flatten slightly at the top to form a wedge. Flatten slightly at the base and indent with the Dresden tool in a circular movement to form a small depression. Leave to dry, then dust with dark brown to give a 'dirty' brown colour.

21 Make a husk for one or two of the nuts. Roll out some of the paste thinly and cut a 2.5cm (1 in) wide strip. Cut into the top as shown and indent with a piece of dried corn husk to create texture. Wrap the husk around the base of the nut. Fold some of the points backwards away from the nut to create a realistic effect. Leave to dry. Dust the husk with dark brown from the base up and also the edges of the points.

22 ACORN: To make the cup, colour a grape-size piece of flower paste brown/grey colour and roll into a small ball. Insert the medium ball tool and flatten the top edge against the thumb. Hook and insert a 26-gauge wire. Make a ball smaller than a grape pip and push into

place over the hooked wire. Pinch tiny marks with tweezers all around the cup. Leave to dry, then dust 'dirty' brown as above (step 20).

23 Colour a large pea-size piece of flower paste a warm brown with chestnut and tartrazine-free cream paste colourings. Roll into an elongated ball and place in the cup so that it fits snugly. Roll a tiny piece of brown stem-wrap and insert into the top of the acorn. Glaze with gum arabic.

TO FINISH

24 Place the gelatine crystals in a small polythene bag. Sprinkle on some brown dusting powder and shake the bag well. These crystals can now be used to represent soil. Pipe a little soft peak royal icing onto the inner base of the flowerpot and over the inner join. Sprinkle the 'earth' onto the icing. Push a cob nut and acorn into the icing. Dust the flowerpot inside and out with dark brown to make it slightly dirty. Pipe some white icing onto the outside join of the flowerpot. Place in position on the cake and attach the mouse. Thin some royal icing to run-out consistency (see page 8) and pipe over and around the flowerpot. Place the leaves, berries and nuts in position as shown.

25 To make the Garrett frill, knead the pastes together, cut and attach around the base of the cake. Lift the frill up at one side and attach a spray of holly, acorns and dried leaves with royal icing. Dust the frilled edge with cream dusting powder, then pipe tiny dots of royal icing along the upper edge of the frill. Fix the ribbon around the cake board to finish.

flowerpot base

robin's coat

tail

Actual size

Poinsettia

*A simple but stunning cake – the gelatine plaque
is decorated with cut-out leaves and poinsettias.*

CAKE AND DECORATIONS

20cm (8 in) square cake
boiled, sieved apricot jam (jelly)
1.25kg (2¹/₂lb) marzipan (almond paste)
1.25kg (2¹/₂lb) bought red sugarpaste
60g (2oz) royal icing
gelatine paste (see page 8)
75g (2¹/₂oz) flower paste
strong red powder colour
*Christmas, gooseberry and spruce green paste
    colourings*
gum arabic (see page 8)
*dark brown, red and forest green dusting powders
    (petal dusts)*

EQUIPMENT

15cm (6 in) round plaque cutter
template (see page 74)
28cm (11 in) square cake board
scriber
scalpel
poinsettia veiner
small ball tool
ivy and holly veiners
cocktail stick (toothpick)
parchment piping bag and No. 1 piping tube (tip)
2m (2yd) thin green ribbon for cake
1.5m (1¹/₂yd) green ribbon for cake board

1   Cover the cake with marzipan and red sugarpaste. Using the plaque cutter, remove a 15cm (6 in) circle of paste from the centre while still soft; leave to dry. Cover the cake board with red sugarpaste; leave to dry. Attach the cake to the board with a little royal icing. Make a gelatine plaque using the same cutter; leave to dry thoroughly.

2   Using the template, scribe the design onto the gelatine plaque. Colour 30g (1oz) flower paste with strong red powder colour and 15g (¹/₂oz) each with Christmas, gooseberry and spruce green paste colourings. Roll out some red paste thinly and, using the template as a pattern, cut out the petals for one of the poinsettias. Vein the petals and soften the edges with the ball tool: place the ball tool half on the edge of the petal and ball firmly to give plenty of movement and shape. Attach to the plaque with gum arabic. Cut out the ivy leaves and holly using the same method and green paste. Roll some tiny balls of red paste for the berries. Repeat for the other two flowers.

3   To make the centres of the poinsettias, lighten the remaining gooseberry green paste with some white paste. Form a small grape-size piece into a ball, then roll into a cone. Hollow out the centre with the cocktail stick. Lay the cones on their sides for the first row.

Place further cones below to form a second row, gradually placing them in a more upright position until the final cone is completely upright. Leave to dry. Colour a little royal icing with strong red powder colour and pipe small bulbs into each cone.

4 Dust the poinsettia petals near the centre with dark brown and red. Dust the centre of the ivy leaves with forest green, radiating outwards. Paint the holly with a mixture of Christmas green paste colouring and gum arabic. Leave to dry, then wave the plaque over a steaming kettle for a second to sheen.

5 Apply a little royal icing to the base of the hollow and place the plaque in position. Pipe a snail's trail in red royal icing around the base of the cake and fix the ribbons around the cake and board. Pipe dots above cake ribbons.

Actual size

Noel, Noel

The embroidered effect of the garland on this cake is achieved simply by piping the design directly onto the cake.

CAKE AND DECORATIONS
25 x 20cm (10 x 8 in) oval cake
boiled, sieved apricot jam (jelly)
1.5kg (3lb) marzipan (almond paste)
1.5kg (3lb) bought marine blue sugarpaste
blueberry, emerald, forest, mint and Christmas green,
*   black and yellow paste colourings*
250g (8 oz) royal icing, soft peak consistency
125g (4oz) bought red sugarpaste
1tsp piping gel
strong red powder colour
moss green dusting powder (petal dust)
extra albumen powder (optional)

EQUIPMENT
33 x 28cm (13 x 11 in) oval cake board
18cm (7 in) oval cutter
template (see page 78)
scriber
parchment piping bags and Nos. 1 and 2 piping tubes
*   (tips)*
No. 1 paintbrush
anglepoise lamp
2m (2yd) green ribbon for cake and board

1 Cover the cake with marzipan. Colour the marine blue sugarpaste with blueberry paste colouring to create a more intense blue. Use to cover the cake and board; leave to dry. Attach the cake to the board with a little royal icing.

2 Using the oval cutter, remove a section of blue sugarpaste from the centre of the cake and replace with the red sugarpaste, rolled and cut to shape. Leave to dry thoroughly. Position the template on the top of the cake and scribe the design onto the sugarpaste.

3 Stir the piping gel into the royal icing; this will slow down the setting time, allowing more time to brush the icing into place. Divide the icing into four. Colour one quarter with emerald and mint green and a touch of black, for the holly. Colour a second quarter with Christmas green and a touch of black, for the ivy. Colour the third quarter with strong red powder, for the holly berries. Leave the remainder white for the Christmas roses and Noel.

4 Fill a piping bag with a little of the holly green and another with the ivy green. Starting on the leaves furthest away and gradually working forwards, outline the leaf using a No. 2 tube. Brush the icing towards the centre. Draw a line down the centre with the brush to form the vein. Using the white icing, shape the petals of the Christmas roses in the same way, brushing the icing towards the centre of the flower. For the holly berries, thin the icing to run-out consistency (see page 8) and pipe a small bulb shape. Dry small sections under the lamp as you work so that the icing dries with a sheen. Leave to dry completely when finished.

5 Dust the centre of the flowers with pale moss green from the centre outwards. Pipe yellow stamens on the flowers and black rough dots on the holly berries with the No. 1 tube.

6   Pipe around NOEL with white royal icing, then flood the letters with run-out icing (see page 8) and the No. 1 tube. Ease the icing into the corners with the paintbrush. Dry under the lamp.

7   Colour some icing with blueberry paste colouring. Using the No. 1 tube, pipe a snail's trail around the base of the cake. Leave to dry, then attach the ribbon. Fix the ribbon around the cake board to finish.

NOTE: NOEL can be piped directly onto the cake or, if preferred, piped as a run-out and transferred to the cake when dry.

Enlarge by 139% on a photocopier

Robin Redbreast

This is a cake for artists. The design is painted directly onto a sugarpaste plaque on top of the cake and the inset is a painted gelatine plaque.

CAKE AND DECORATIONS

18 x 28cm (7 x 11 in) rectangular cake
boiled, sieved apricot jam (jelly)
1.25kg (2¹/₂lb) marzipan (almond paste)
1.75kg (3¹/₂lb) sugarpaste
brown, mint and spruce green paste colourings
60g (2oz) royal icing
60g (2oz) modelling paste
gelatine paste (see page 8)
green and brown dusting powders (petal dusts)

EQUIPMENT

25 x 36cm (10 x 14 in) rectangular cake board
templates (see below and page 80)
12.5 x 8cm (5 x 3¹/₄ in) oval plaque cutter
scriber
Nos. 00 and 1 paintbrushes
parchment piping bag and No. 1 piping tube (tip)
3.5m (3¹/₂yd) thin green ribbon for cake
1.5m (1¹/₂yd) green ribbon for cake board

Enlarge by 118% on a photocopier

1 Cover the cake with marzipan. Colour 1.25kg (2¹/₂lb) sugarpaste with a little mint green and spruce green paste colourings to create an *eau de nil* colour. Use to cover the cake. Cover the cake board with white sugarpaste; leave to dry. Attach the cake to the board with a little royal icing.

2 Mix the modelling paste with the remaining white sugarpaste and roll out thinly. Using the template, cut out the rectangular plaque and attach to the cake while still soft. Using the plaque cutter, remove an oval piece of paste from the centre while still soft. Make a gelatine plaque using the same cutter. Leave all to dry thoroughly.

3 Using the robin template, scribe the design onto the plaque, then paint (see Note). The success of the plaque depends on the subtle blending of various green and brown colours on each leaf, as shown overleaf.

4 Use the scriber or the point of a scalpel to create the fine veins on the leaves. Scratch fine lines onto the painted robin to soften the edges of defined areas, e.g.

red breast and white underbelly. This technique will also create the essential feathery effect.

5   Scribe and paint the leaf design on the white plaque as before.

6   Apply a little royal icing to the base of the hollow and place the painted plaque in position. Pipe a snail's trail around the base of the cake. Fix ribbons to the cake and board as shown.

NOTE: When painting on sugarpaste, keep the brush fairly dry. Too much moisture will create streaking and will also melt the sugar. Subtle blending of colours can be achieved by brushing one colour into the next while still wet. To lift colour from the plaque, wet the brush slightly, place it over the area of colour to be lifted, remove and clean the brush with a tissue. Re-apply the now dry brush over the same area. This should reduce the colour to a much lighter tone. If clearly defined shapes are to be produced, leave one colour to dry completely before an adjacent colour, surface pattern or veining is applied.

Enlarge by 130% on a photocopier

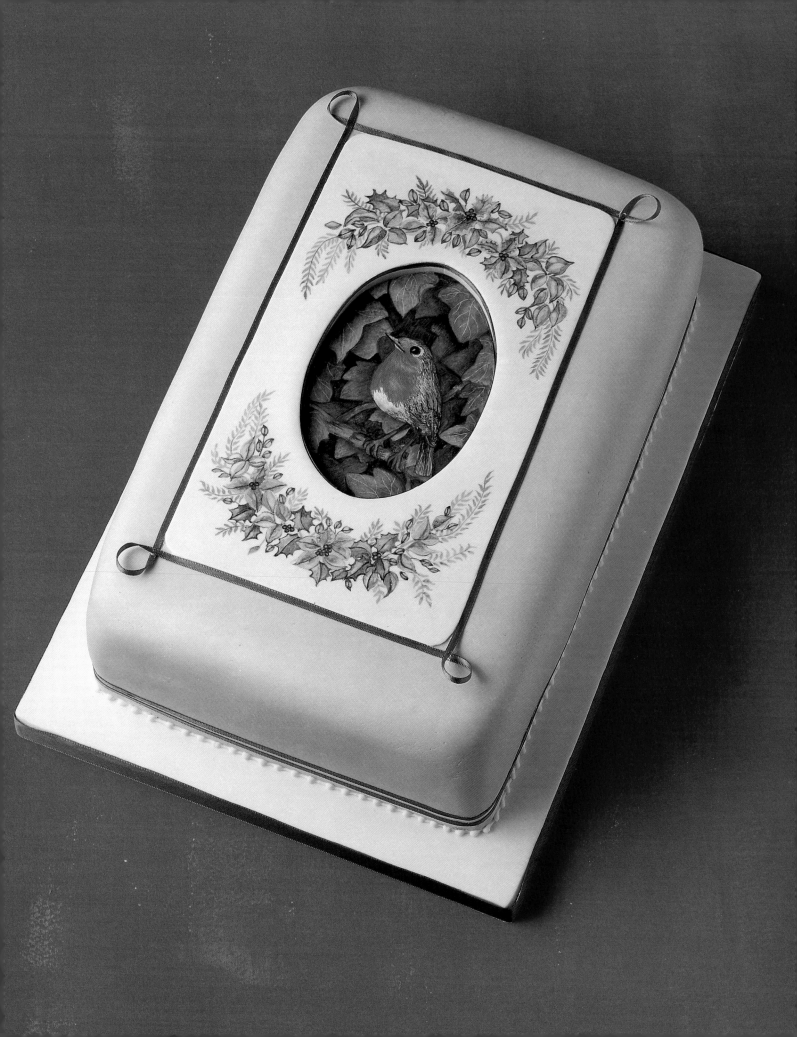

Christmas Tree

This tree is cut from a slab cake and decorated with a mix of cut-out, moulded and shaped decorations.

CAKE AND DECORATIONS

20cm (8 in) square slab cake
boiled, sieved apricot jam (jelly)
1kg (2lb) marzipan (almond paste)
1.75kg (3½lb) sugarpaste
Christmas green, dark brown, paprika, melon, black and
    tartrazine-free cream paste colourings
185g (6oz) modelling paste
60g (2oz) royal icing
burgundy and pillar box red strong powder colours
gum arabic (see page 8)
cream and gold dusting powders (petal dusts)
cornflour (cornstarch) for dusting
gold and silver food colourings

EQUIPMENT

templates (see page 94)
36 x 40cm (14 x 16 in) rectangular cake board
doll's head (for mould)
cocktail sticks (toothpicks)
scalpel
No. 00 paintbrush
parchment piping bag and No. 1 piping tube (tip)
Dresden tool
pieces of dowel
small ball tool
small palette knife
pieces of foam
small bell mould
medium plunger cutter
2m (2yd) red ribbon for cake board

1   Using the template provided, cut the cake into the tree shape. Cover with marzipan. Colour 1kg (2lb) sugarpaste with Christmas green paste colouring and use to cover the cake. Cover the board with white sugarpaste; leave to dry. Attach the cake to the board, leaving enough space to attach the tub to the base of the tree.

2   Colour 90g (3oz) sugarpaste with dark brown paste colouring, roll out thinly and cut out the tub, using the template. Attach to the base of the tree. Mark in the wood texture with the sharp edge of an ordinary knife. Cut out and fix darker brown strips to represent iron bands.

ANGEL

3   HEAD: colour 15g (½oz) modelling paste with a little paprika and a touch of melon to create a skintone colour. Use a doll's head to make a mould and head (see Eskimo, page 30). Insert a cocktail stick into each nostril. Cut between the lips with the scalpel to open. Place the head on a cocktail stick and paint on the features. Colour a small amount of royal icing a light golden brown using cream and dark brown paste colourings. Pipe onto the head to represent hair.

4   DRESS: Colour a large grape-size piece of modelling paste with the strong burgundy powder colour. Leave for a few minutes for the depth of colour to be achieved. Make a large ball, then roll to form an elongated round cone. The top of the cone will form the shoulders so do not roll into a point. Open up the base of the cone with the end of the paintbrush to thin out and frill. Form crease lines in the skirt with the point of the Dresden tool. Roll the cone between the two index fingers, one-third down from the shoulders, to form the waist. Mark in the creases for the upper bodice with the Dresden tool. Place on a piece of dowel to dry. Roll out a long fine strand of white modelling paste, making the ends pointed. Wrap around the upper body, criss-crossing in front and taking around the waist. Butt together in front and let fall down and open. Leave to dry, then paint gold.

5   ARMS: Roll a pea-size piece of flesh-coloured modelling paste into a sausage. Flatten one end between thumb and finger. Cut out a wedge, as shown, to create a thumb. As the hand is small there is no need to create fingers – simply curl to look natural. To form a wrist, roll the paste between the fingers. Continue to roll and pinch out an elbow. Bend the arm and cut away a wedge on the inside of the upper arm so that it will sit well when attached to the body. Leave to dry. Roll out a little burgundy paste and cut a rough sleeve shape. Wrap around the upper arm and cut away the excess. Leave to dry. Attach the arms and head to the body with a little paste colouring mixed with gum arabic to form a sticky 'glue'.

6   WINGS: Roll out a grape-size piece of white modelling paste thinly. Using the template, carefully cut around the wings. Soften the cut edge with the ball tool. Mark the division between the feathers with the edge of

the palette knife. Curve and support the wings with foam and leave to dry. Paint fine grey lines onto the feathers as shown, using black paste colouring. Dust the edges of the wings with cream and gold dusting powders. Leave to dry. Attach the wings to the cake board with a little royal icing. Place the angel on the wings and attach with royal icing.

BELLS

7   Shape a medium grape-size piece of modelling paste into a cone. Open up the end with a piece of dowel. Dust the outside with cornflour and drop into the mould. Continue to push the paste against the mould with the fingers until satisfied with the thinness of the paste. Cut away the excess around the bottom of the bell. Using the scalpel, cut in half while still in the mould. Leave to dry, then remove from the mould and paint gold. Make ten bells and attach to the cake with royal icing (see main picture).

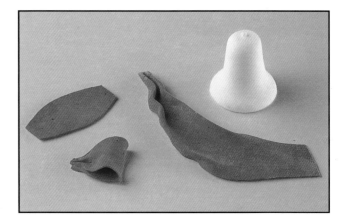

ASSORTED BAUBLES

8   To make simple balls or elongated baubles, roll pea-size pieces of modelling paste into balls, then simply tease the paste out at the base by tweaking and

pinching. Elongate by rolling between index fingers. Cut away a slice at the back of each bauble so that they will sit on the cake. Place on cocktail sticks to hold more easily and paint various patterns of your choice.

9 To make the silver clasp, use a medium plunger cutter to create the shape. Rotate on the inside with the ball tool to exaggerate the cup shape. Paint silver and leave to dry. Attach to the top of the bauble with a dot of royal icing. Roll a thin strand of modelling paste and attach to the top of the bauble to form a ring. Leave to dry, then paint silver.

DRAPES AND BOWS

10 Colour 90g (3oz) modelling paste with pillar box red powder colour. Leave for a few minutes for the shade to deepen. Using the templates, cut out each drape. Soften the cut edges with the ball tool. Fold under the top and bottom edges. Form into folds using a cocktail stick and Dresden tool. Attach to the cake with gum arabic (see main picture). Trim and flatten the edge where the bow is to be attached so that it will sit neatly.

11 Using the templates, cut out all the bow shapes in red paste, soften the cut edges and attach with gum arabic. Attach the baubles to the cake with royal icing.

Using red modelling paste form a fine strand. Thread through the silver ring on the bauble to form a circle. Attach another fine strand in a figure of eight. Shape to form a bow and fix to the cake with gum arabic.

PRESENTS

12 Make an assortment of simple parcels and presents in modelling paste. Cut away part of the back so that each shape will sit at the correct angle under the tree. Make in white or a pastel colour and paint on an interesting wrapping paper design or decorate with a ribbon or bow. Fix the ribbon around the cake board to finish.

Templates

Unless otherwise specified in the instructions, all templates should be made with good quality tracing paper. The drawings are the author's own originals and may vary slightly in detail from the finished cakes.

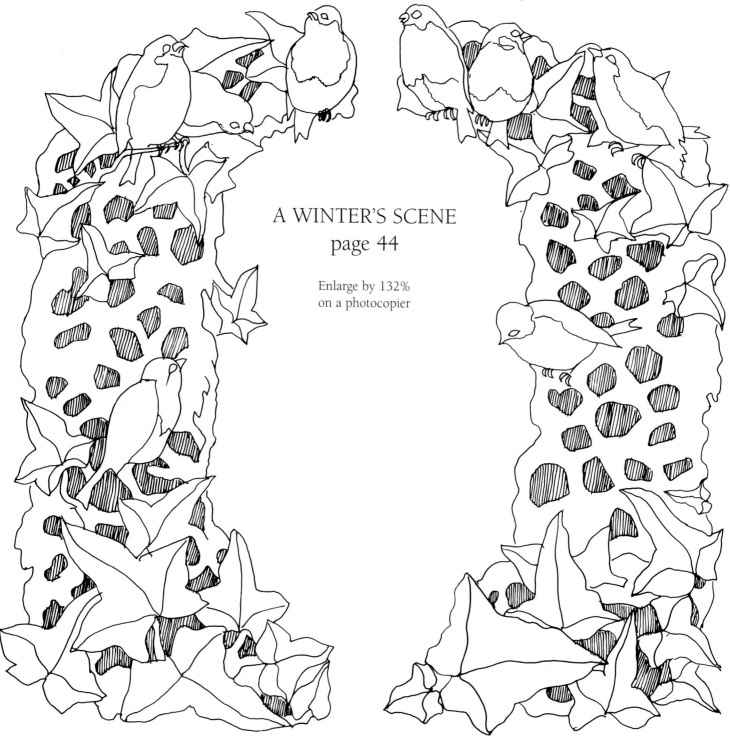

A WINTER'S SCENE
page 44

Enlarge by 132%
on a photocopier

left side of collar

right side of collar

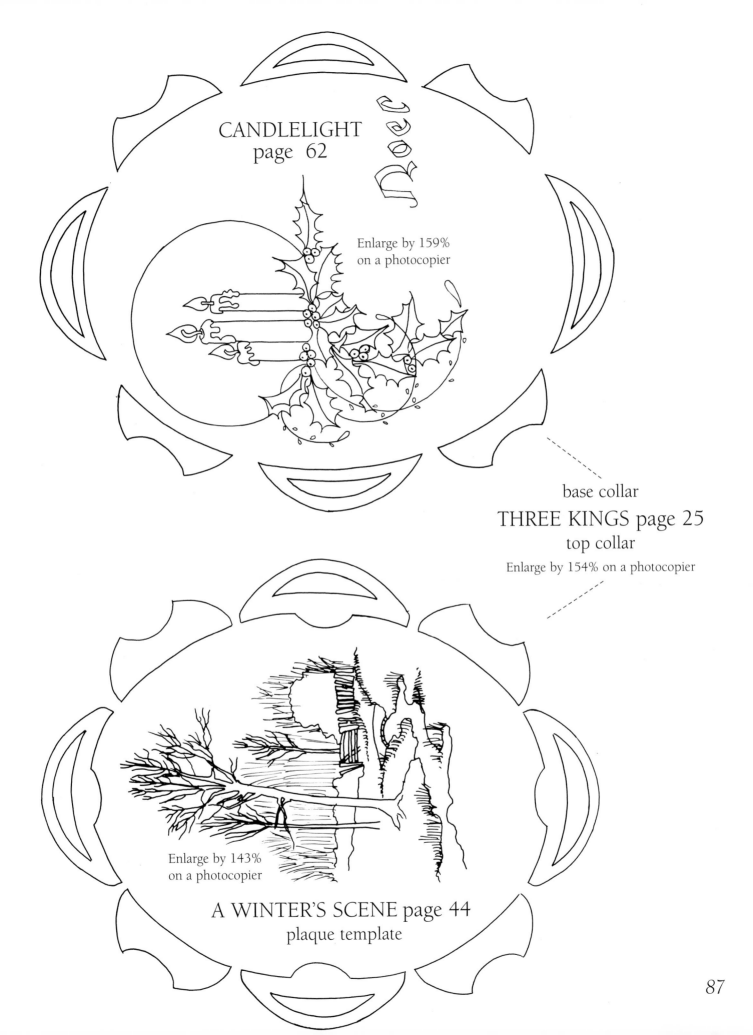

CANDLELIGHT
page 62

Noel

Enlarge by 159%
on a photocopier

base collar

THREE KINGS page 25
top collar

Enlarge by 154% on a photocopier

Enlarge by 143%
on a photocopier

A WINTER'S SCENE page 44
plaque template

THE NATIVITY page 16

Enlarge by 118% on a photocopier

Roof

support for roof

support for roof

base plaque

upright support

fence

Joseph's sleeve

Mary's face
and hand

Joseph's
hand

baby's head and body

crib

lower sleeve

Mary's veil
and dress

THE NATIVITY page 16
border outlines
Enlarge by 118% on a photocopier

Enlarge by 111%
on a photocopier

CHRISTMAS GARLAND page 22

89

Enlarge by 115%
on a photocopier

FESTIVE ROBINS page 59
top collar template

CHRISTMAS
MANGER
page 36

Enlarge by 115%
on a photocopier

FESTIVE ROBINS page 59
base collar template

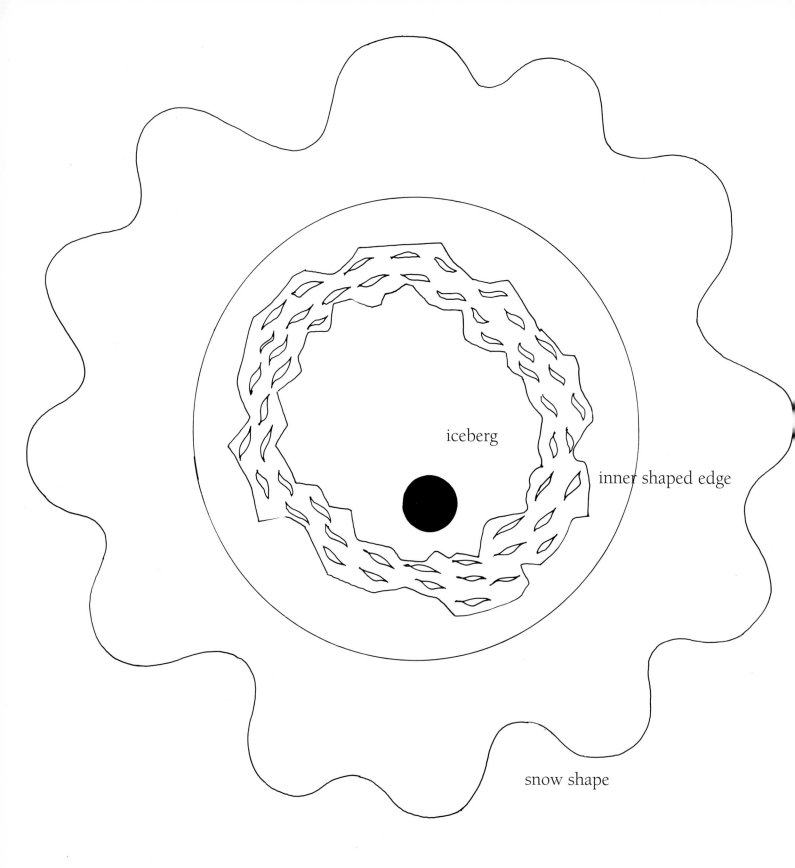

iceberg

inner shaped edge

snow shape

ESKIMO CAKE page 28

Enlarge by 152% on a photocopier

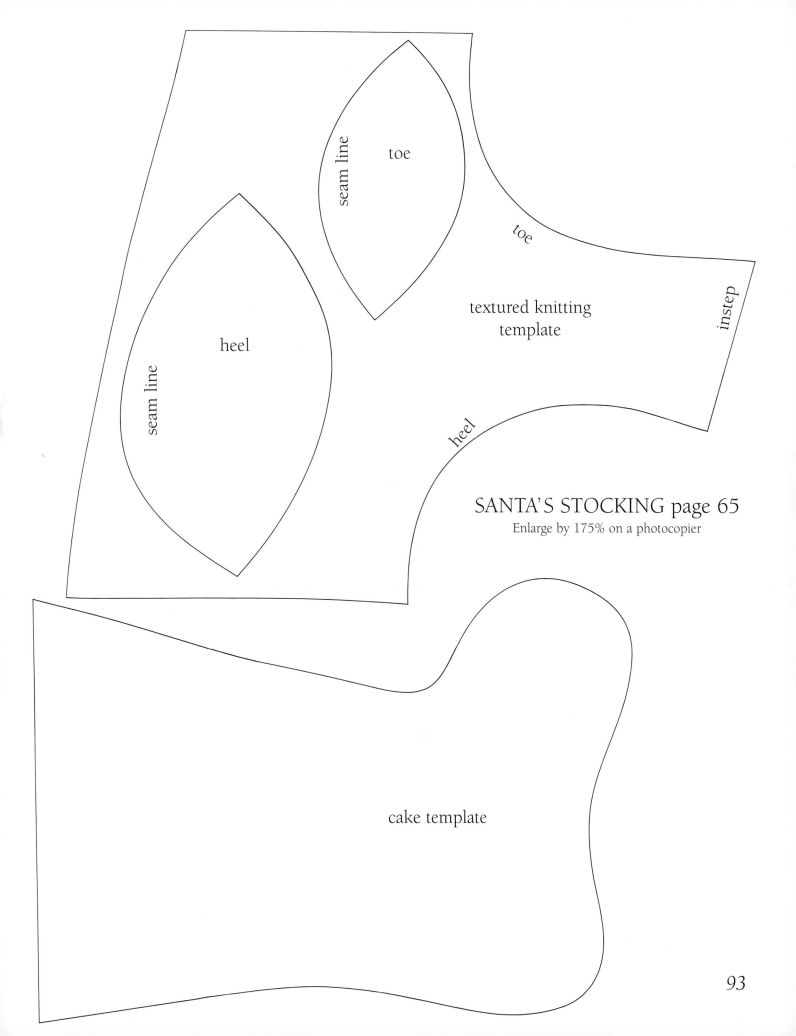

seam line

toe

toe

instep

heel

seam line

heel

textured knitting
template

SANTA'S STOCKING page 65

Enlarge by 175% on a photocopier

cake template

93

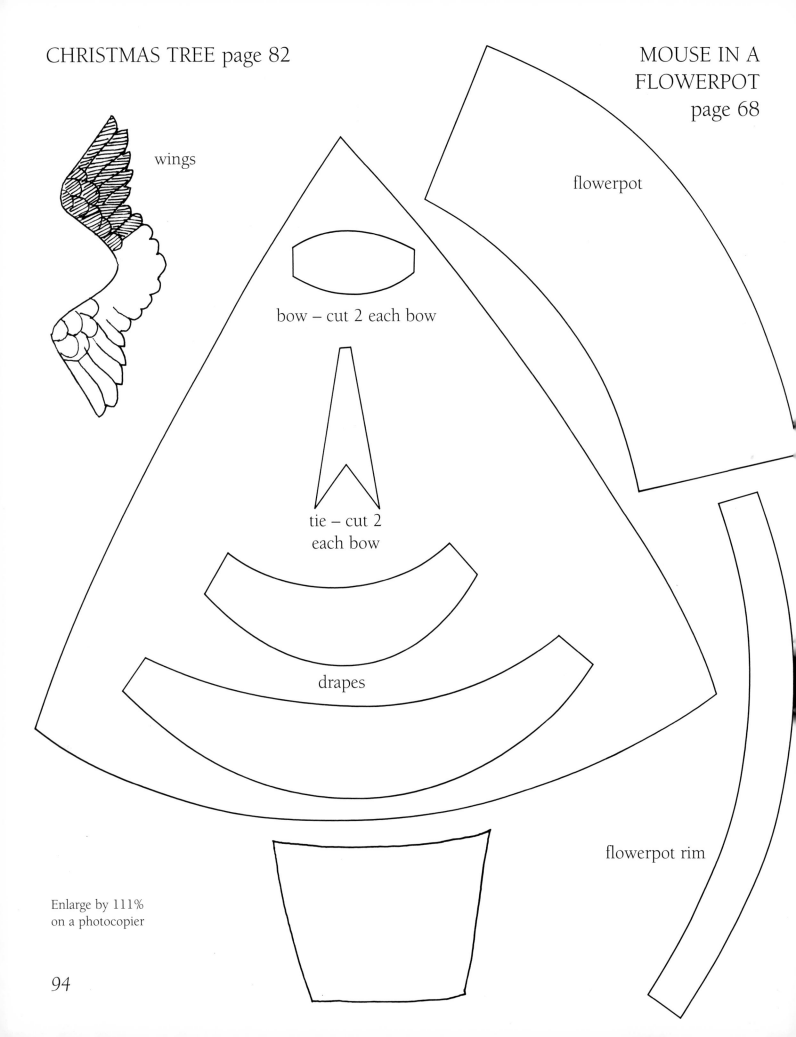

wings

flowerpot

bow – cut 2 each bow

tie – cut 2
each bow

drapes

flowerpot rim

Enlarge by 111%
on a photocopier

overlapping base shape

Index

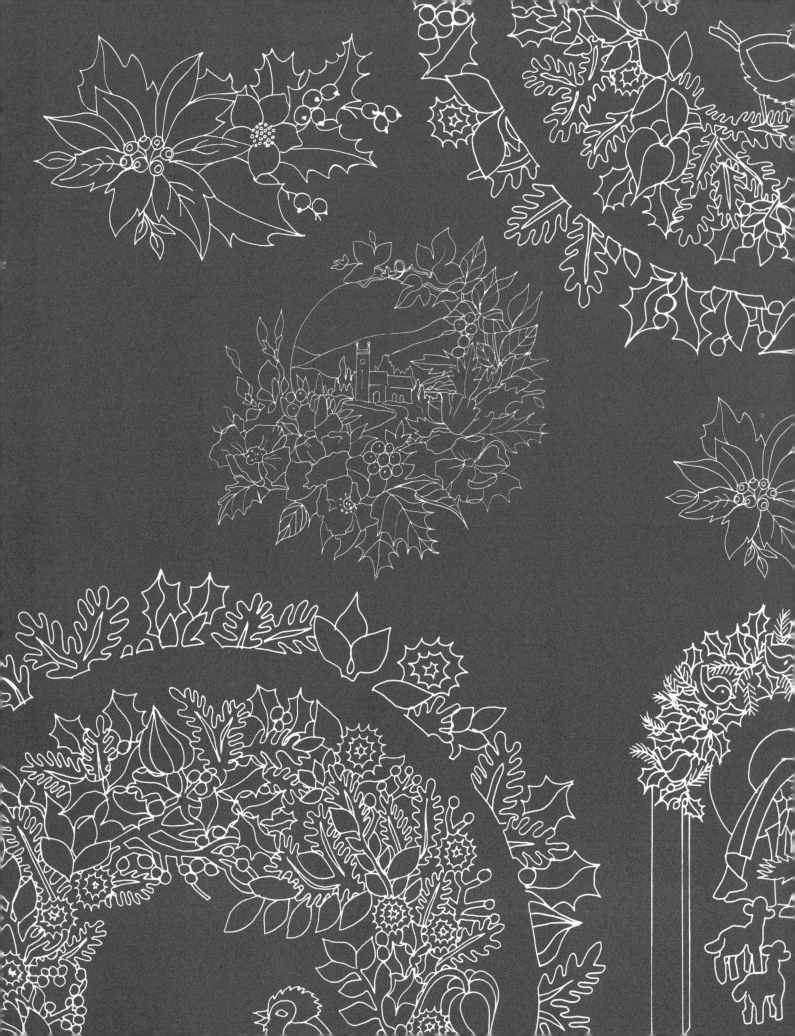